I am deeply grateful to every rug artist who sent me flowers and allowed their offerings to be shared on these pages. The magnificent and unique floral rugs in the pages of Rugs in Bloom *will inspire rug hookers to plant their own special gardens on rug foundations across the world.*

Toni Breeding	Julie Gibson	Barbara Jess	Jane Olsen	Gene Shepherd
Elissa Crouch	Margaret Grabus	Betty Kerr	Suzanne Pastura	Ruth Mills Smith
Sally D'Albora	Linda Gustafson	Ruth Ladd	Sarah Province	Jeanne Sullivan
Claire DeRoos	Carol Fields Hagen	Cindy MacIntosh	Nancy Lee Ross	JoAnn Strickland
Ginny Fan	Marian Hall	Nancy MacLennan	Abbie Ross	Marian Thompson
Jeanne Field	Jacqueline Hansen	Tassey Mariani	Pat Seliga	Helen Vance
Jane McGown Flynn	Jo Ann Hendrix	Kathy Meentemeyer	Kate H. Senger	Lissa Williamson
Lynn Fowler	Ingrid Hieronimus	Cyndra Mogayzel	Marc Senger	

Special thanks to my daughter Kate Senger who was

the first person to read the book and help edit the final copy.

I love my husband Don, the real gardener in the family,

who supported me and offered botanical advice along the way.

Finally I would like to thank Debra Smith, editor of *Rug Hooking*

magazine, for her expert guidance throughout this project

and for giving me another opportunity to write a book about

one of my favorite subjects.

TABLE OF CONTENTS

Rugs in Bloom

Shading Flowers in Hooked Rugs

JANE HALLIWELL GREEN

Copyright © 2012 by Stackpole Books
Published by
STACKPOLE BOOKS
5067 Ritter Road
Mechanicsburg, PA 17055
www.stackpolebooks.com

Customer Service (877) 462-2604
www.rughookingmagazine.com

On the front cover: *Day Lilies*, Jane Halliwell Green
On the back cover: *Dancing Cyclamen*, Jane Halliwell Green

Illustrations by Jane Halliwell Green
Photographs by Impact Xpozures, unless otherwise noted
Cover design by Caroline M. Stover

Library of Congress Cataloging-in-Publication Data

Green, Jane Halliwell
Rugs in bloom: shading flowers in hooked rugs / Jane Halliwell Green.— p. cm.
    ISBN 978-1-881982-78-4
    1. Rugs, Hooked. 2. Flowers in art. I. Title.
    TT850.G653 2012
    746.7'4—dc23
2011045157

Rapture Plus Four, *detail. See full rug on page 128–129.*

Jane Halliwell Green began hooking rugs when she was ten years old at the urging of her Irish grandmother. An unfinished rug always stood at the entrance to her grandmother's New England home, and the only way she and the other grandchildren were allowed passage into the kitchen was to hook a few loops. It was years later, back in 1988, that she remembered her grandmother's rugs and fell in love with the art of rug hooking again.

Jane teaches classes and workshops in the United States and Canada and was the first rug hooking instructor to teach at the Smithsonian Institute in Washington, D.C. She served on the editorial board of *Rug Hooking* magazine for many years and contributed many articles for publication. She wrote two books, *The Pictorial Rug* (Stackpole 2000) and *Pictorial Hooked Rugs* (Stackpole 2009). In 2002 she returned to school, and in 2005, she graduated from the Ringling School of Art and Design in Sarasota, Florida, with a certificate of fine arts.

Jane's specialties are pictorial rugs and floral rugs. She researched and developed a simple color theory based on a color clock, which she teaches frequently. Jane sells hand-dyed "designer wools" to rug hookers in the United States and Canada.

Jane lives in Edgewater, Maryland with her husband, Don, and their dog, Sage. They have five grown children. She teaches locally at Anne Arundel Community College, Chesapeake College, and Maryland Hall for The Arts, and she travels around the country to teach rug hooking. Jane is an accomplished painter and signature member of the Baltimore Watercolor Society.

Visit her websites at *www.rugandwool.com* and *www.paintpencil.com.*

My mother, Kay Halliwell, was an avid gardener. I hold her responsible for my early love of flowers. Our home was always filled with cut flowers in the spring and summer. As a little girl I looked forward to the first lily of the valley in the spring and the multicolored zinnias in the summer.

Flowers represent a universal language that brings us together. The *Friendship Rug* shown here is a good example. Karen Rose designed the rug, and although it belongs to JoAnn Strickland, almost a dozen rug hookers participated in creating it.

Flowers are a part of our lives during happy and sad times. Poets have been inspired by them and countries have adopted particular blossoms as their own. The rug hooking community has always embraced the subject and made the floral rug one of the most common designs around.

In fiber art, we have a multitude of ways to create flowers—from the simple rose that is outlined and filled to the finely shaded chrysanthemum. In *Rugs in Bloom*, I want to show not only examples of these traditional favorites, but also to add blooms with a contemporary twist. Rug hookers today are true artists who desire expression of their individual visions. This will undoubtedly lead to the growth of rug hooking as an art form in the decades ahead.

Rugs in Bloom was designed to be the type of book I would want to own in order to better understand how fiber flowers are created. This book is a serious reference resource. It will teach you how to hook more than forty different blooms. Each blossom is carefully described by its color, shape, botanical name, and distinguishing characteristics. Each flower is rated by difficulty to help new fiber artists select a project. As you will see, the diagrams in this book are all in grayscale. Though different from recent books on flowers, this style was used in the 1950s by our grandmothers. It is the best tool to visualize and render the shape of a flower accurately. ✑

Friendship Rug, 26" x 23", *wool on linen. Designed by Karen Rose and hooked by Trude Myers (columbine), Maxine Gallagher (daisy), Julie Gibson (fuchsia), Boo Kapowitz (lily of the valley), Barbara Personette (bird of paradise), Karen Rose (iris), Mary Tyez (rose and rosebud), JoAnn Strickland (hibiscus), Leslie Cushnie (Queen Anne's lace), June Britton (pansy), and Marion Thompson (tulip). Owned by JoAnn Strickland, Fairfax, Virginia, 2010.*

HOW TO USE THIS BOOK

Groups of flowers share similar structures; therefore, the flower chapters are organized by shape. A geometric representation of this shape will appear on the first page of each chapter. Although the colors and individual markings differ from one plant to another, the basic shape and hooking technique for these shapes are alike. Some flowers are a combination of shapes. For example, the daffodil is part trumpet and part ellipse. In these cases, the flowers are categorized based on the shape that is the most dominant within its structure.

In this book, a flower's shape is presented in generic fashion without a particular pose. In nature, however, flowers assume poses. The pose is part of what gives the flower its personality. For instance, a tulip may appear to grow upright in an illustration, but in nature it will bend and twist or perhaps have other flowers or leaves overlapping it. After mastering the hooking of a flower in its generic form, place it in a unique pose and try it again. Anything painters can achieve in rendering flowers can also be done in fiber art.

Each flower is identified by its common plant name, with its genus, or botanical name, in parentheses. This detail is important because some flowers are better known by their botanical name. If you are familiar with both, you will always be able to research the plant.

Each flower will be described in detail. A single flower may have hundreds of versions depending on the variety. Study the version you want to hook in depth. To capture that flower's personality, you will need to include as many of its distinguishing characteristics as possible. For this reason, I include the following content headings in chapters seven through thirteen.

Color. The familiar colors of each flower are listed. Some flowers have an unlimited palette of color while others are limited, sometimes only to one or two colors.

Petals. The number of petals, their shape, and any special characteristics often help to identify a flower.

Flower centers. Sometimes the flower center is the masterpiece. A good example is a sunflower. If you get the center right and miss some detail in the petals, everyone will still know it is a sunflower.

Leaves and stems. Refer to this section for the wide range of leaf shapes and edges. However, do not expect color guidance; leaves are multicolored!

Rating. Use this difficulty scale, with 1 being an easy flower to hook and 10 being the most difficult. A rating of 1–3 is a good choice for a new rug hooker; 4–6 is a good choice for someone who has hooked a few years; 7–10 represents difficult flowers best tackled by experienced rug hookers.

Challenge. Here you will find a forewarning of potential obstacles. Knowing about these challenges in advance will prepare you to master them.

Materials. Most flowers are handled with a dip dye, swatch, or combination of the two. The first choice listed is the preferred one.

How to hook. Because each flower is unique, special hooking instructions will be included for each plant. Some of the flowers are broken down into two hooking methods: primitive or realistic. If the primitive approach is not included then it is not appropriate for that flower.

Dye formulas. Formulas that are ideal for a particular flower will be listed frequently, but not for every flower. Look to the resource section at the back of this book for more information.

Illustrations. In previous rug hooking books about flower shading, small numbers were used to indicate color values. Instead of using numbers, I chose shaded pencil drawings to show the correct values in a more intuitive way. The value scale is in chapter three.

A second ink drawing accompanies the shaded drawing on each page. The arrows indicate in what direction to hook. In addition, the letters L (light), M (medium), and D (dark) appear when additional clarification about values would help. A dotted red line signifies an area where a darker value is required and where it may be necessary to skip values in order to shape the flower. Numbers indicate the order of hooking.

When possible, I have included a hooked example of the flower.

My hope is that keeping this book by your side will plant the seeds of new ideas. I can't wait to see all of the new designs that bloom forth in the years ahead. —Jane Halliwell Green

CHAPTER ONE

Floral Rugs Past and Present

Roses and Pansies Antique, 27" x 39", #4-cut wool on linen.
Designed and hooked by Jacqueline Hansen, Scarborough, Maine, 1999. BERNADETTE BOLDUCPAPI

Flowers have been an endless source of inspiration for rug hookers since the early part of the nineteenth century. The top three hooked rug designs of that time period were animals, houses, and flowers. Everyone loved flowers; they were a universal subject, and part of the human experience was—and still is—to seek a connection to the natural world. Because of this connection, flowers have been used symbolically through history. Almost any flower has meaning, whether it is the love expressed by a red rose or the long life that is associated with chrysanthemums.

Early hooked rugs were predominant in the

> *"When tranquility is disturbed and the pace of life quickens beyond endurance, go to your frame and hook. You'll be surprised at how many problems have been solved with a hook."* —Pearl McGown

1

Erin, *27" x 44", #3-cut wool on cotton warp cloth.*
Designed for House of Price (#1546) and hooked by Jane McGown Flynn, Center Harbor, New Hampshire, 2011. NANCY BASS

My English Garden, *30½" x 46"*
Designed and hooked by Jeanne Field, Aurora, Ontario, Canada, 1991. ANDREA FIELD

Kashan Roses, *27" x 39", #3- and 4-cut wool on monk's cloth.*
Designed and hooked by Jane Olsen, Hawthorne, California, 2000. GENE SHEPHERD

Canadian Provinces and in New England. One of the earliest examples of nineteenth century hooked floral rugs can be found in the Waldoboro collections, named after the town of Waldoboro, Maine, where the style developed. These rug designs featured central ovals, borders, florals, baskets, and leaf and scroll motifs that were sculpted—either clipped or unclipped—and rested on a black background. This technique yielded a three-dimensional finished piece. Jacqueline Hansen is an expert in this style of hooked rug. The rug, *Roses and Pansies Antique*, is a wonderful example of a Waldoboro style rug.

Fantasy Flower,
15" x 18", #5-cut wool on linen. Designed by Jane Halliwell Green, Edgewater, Maryland, and hooked by Nancy Lee Ross, Hinesburg, Vermont, 2010. NANCY LEE ROSS

In the early part of the twentieth century, Pearl McGown emerged as a strong force in the rug hooking world. Pearl, who was first a designer, then a teacher, and finally a teacher's teacher, introduced fiber artists to "painting with wool." Her prime subjects were finely hooked florals surrounded by elaborate scrolls. Prior to Pearl's arrival, the majority of hooked rugs were primitive florals hooked with whatever rags were available in the home. Not only did Pearl introduce the concept of preplanning a rug, but she also brought to the forefront the technique of dyeing wool in many values of color to create a more realistic floral.

Pearl wrote many books including *Color in Hooked Rugs, You Can Hook Rugs, The Dreams Beneath Design,* and *The Lore and Lure of Hooked Rugs.* Her granddaughter, Jane McGown Flynn, has continued the family tradition by naming rugs for her grand- and great-grandchildren. Jane designed and hooked the rug *Erin* for her granddaughter, Erin. Traditional rug hooking owes both Jane and Pearl a debt of gratitude for the legacy they have created, particularly in the area of the design and teaching of the floral rug.

Two other individuals who have made major contributions to rug hooking, particularly floral rugs, are Jeanne Field and Jane Olsen. Jeanne wrote *Shading with Flowers*, published in 1991, a valuable resource on the subject of hooking flowers for two decades. Jane authored the popular newsletter, *Ruggers Roundtable,* which she distributed for many years. In their long and esteemed careers both have inspired unknown numbers of rug hookers.

Rugs in Bloom will show step by step how to create both the finely shaded and primitive floral rug. It takes a step forward by featuring flowers less familiar to the rug hooking community. It includes shaded, wide-cut wall hangings and examples of flowers hooked in a traditional manner yet designed with imagination and presented in a unique setting. These rugs will inspire you to discover new and exciting ways to portray the millions of potential blossoms found in nature.

A fear of fine shading and the desire for perfection keeps many rug hookers away from the subject of florals. Once you have used a simple set of values to shade one flower, you will clearly see how the same principles apply broadly to virtually all flowers: the shape of the flower changes, not the technique. You will also find that the past emphasis on achieving perfect color—using a certain green because it is the closest match to a real leaf—is unnecessary. Give up perfection and have some fun instead! Most flowers come in many hues, and leaves can be hooked in a variety of colors despite their botanical description. Take a look at the fanciful flowers—with no connection to nature—that were hooked by Nancy Lee Ross and Suzanne Pastura. ✑

Fantasy Flower, *15" x 18", #5-cut wool on linen. Designed by Jane Halliwell Green, Edgewater, Maryland, and hooked by Suzanne Pastura, Annandale, Virginia, 2011.*

CHAPTER TWO

Flower Anatomy

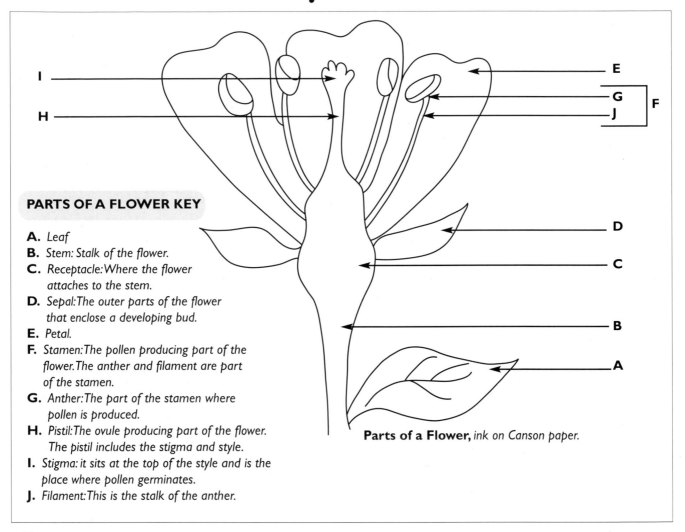

PARTS OF A FLOWER KEY

A. Leaf

B. Stem: Stalk of the flower.

C. Receptacle: Where the flower attaches to the stem.

D. Sepal: The outer parts of the flower that enclose a developing bud.

E. Petal.

F. Stamen: The pollen producing part of the flower. The anther and filament are part of the stamen.

G. Anther: The part of the stamen where pollen is produced.

H. Pistil: The ovule producing part of the flower. The pistil includes the stigma and style.

I. Stigma: it sits at the top of the style and is the place where pollen germinates.

J. Filament: This is the stalk of the anther.

Parts of a Flower, ink on Canson paper.

It is not necessary to be a botanist to hook flowers, but a basic understanding of the various parts of a flower is useful. If you can distinguish a sepal from a pistil, the instructions in each chapter will take on greater meaning and allow you to create a more complete depiction of each flower.

The illustration above does not show you the incredible detail of a real flower; it only identifies the major parts. When a flower is broken down into its components, you will see that every petal has its own personality. Some are irregular, and some curled. A crease may appear in one and not another. Feel free to bookmark this diagram and flip back and forth to it until you are comfortable with the terms.

Before using these visual aids, study some real flowers. During the spring and summer, bring flowers into the house and take them apart. Flowers won't last as you hook an entire rug, but there will be enough time to study the parts, take some photographs, and even sketch a few. Look carefully at the flower's unique features and take notes. Notice how the leaves attach to the stem, and get an idea of their general size and shape in comparison to the flower. Feel the stem and other parts to determine their texture. Pay close attention to the flower's center. This extra effort and familiarity builds confidence during the drawing, color planning, and hooking stages. ◌

CHAPTER THREE

Value and Technique

> *"It is at the edge of a petal that Love waits."* —William Carlos Williams

Value

Understanding and mastering value, the key tool used by an artist to render flowers, is imperative. A common phrase is: "Color gets all the credit, but value does all the work." This is particularly true when it comes to shading flowers.

Value is defined as the relative lightness or darkness of a color. This can be as simple as light, medium, and dark, or as complicated as very light, light, medium light, medium, dark, and very dark. The range of values depends on the style of rug (primitive or realistic) and the artist's desired level of detail.

Using the Value Chart

The value chart is the most important tool in this book. This chart is divided into six values from just a hint of color to completely saturated color: tint, light, medium light, medium, dark, and very dark. It is a guide to value placement. The older, more familiar tool that uses numbers to describe values (e.g., 1 for light and 6 for dark) is not used in this book. Instead, numbers indicate the order in which to hook the petals.

My goal is to simplify flower shading. It is important to see the values, not just rely on numbers. This practice will make you a better artist. You may collapse the six values into three (light, medium, and dark) or increase them to eight by adding an additional medium light and a dark.

The placement of values depends upon the design of the rug. Sometimes a flower is hooked with a light edge and a dark interior; other times the order is reversed. In fiber art, it is the background, rather than the light source, that is often the determining factor. Apply the following tips to all flowers:

ℕ When a flower petal is completely exposed, meaning that no other petal overlaps it, it will be lighter. Think of a bunch of grapes: the ones on the top are lighter and you can see the roundness of the grape. As you gaze deeper into the bunch, moving closer to the vine, the fruit is in shadow and you see only a small portion of each grape. When the top grapes are hooked using a tint and the bottom ones are hooked using a dark value, suddenly there is depth. The same principle applies with overlapping flowers. A petal fully exposed so that all edges are clearly visible is the top petal, and therefore, it is the lightest one in the flower.

ℕ A petal barely visible under all the other petals is darker.

ℕ A petal with only one side covered is lighter than one with both edges obscured.

ℕ The space between petals must be darker in order to clearly see the adjoining petals.

ℕ Where a petal bulges it will be lighter.

ℕ Ruffles, creases, turnovers, and turnunders are portrayed by changes in value.

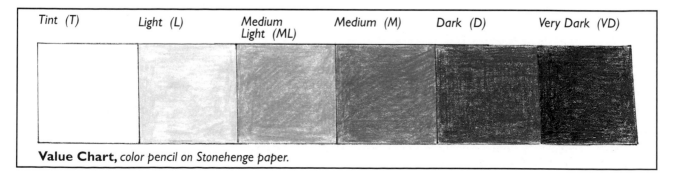

Tint (T)	Light (L)	Medium Light (ML)	Medium (M)	Dark (D)	Very Dark (VD)

Value Chart, *color pencil on Stonehenge paper.*

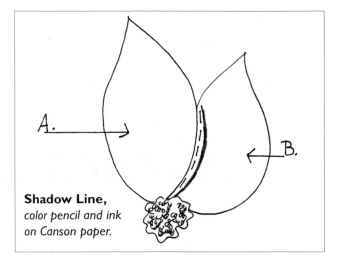

Shadow Line,
color pencil and ink on Canson paper.

plaid outline
Outline and Fill

Dark Background

Flowers assume different poses due to variability in growth patterns. Take this into consideration when selecting the appropriate values.

The flower illustrations in this book represent a flower as it is seen with the sun directly above it. In most cases the edges are light and the area closest to the flower center is darker. If the light source is important, such as in a design featuring a vase of flowers sitting on a windowsill, adjust the values accordingly.

A red dotted line is a reminder that you have a shadow and need to use your darker values. The dotted line appears frequently between petals and near turnovers and petal rolls. In the illustration above, (A) is the lightest top petal and (B) is underneath and partially hidden.

VALUE SKETCHES

Sketching the values in color pencil is easy and provides the perfect road map for hooking. In this book, I used a set of Prismacolor pencils in cool gray. The 10% pencil corresponds to the light value, 30% to medium light, 50% to medium, 70% to dark, and 90% to very dark. Prismacolor pencils are available through any art supply company and most local craft stores.

Techniques for Flower Shading

An artist can shade a simple tulip many ways. The flower's pose is an important consideration. One blossom stands straight and tall, while another falls over and appears to twist—each calls for different shading. Once you master the simple techniques associated with shading, you can apply them to any flower in any pose.

Flower shading is not limited to a narrow #3 cut. Beautiful primitive flowers are created with a limited palette of values. Shaded wide cuts, called *close ups*, use up to eight values with 1" ripped strips! If you are a new rug hooker, hook your first flower using primitive or mock shading techniques before trying a realistic flower. This approach will give you experience in handling a limited number of values.

Primitive Shading

Primitive shading is the simplest type of shading. Each petal is outlined with a plaid or tweed fabric and filled with a light, medium, or dark value. This might be a

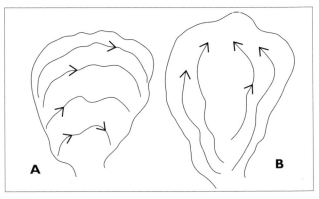

Mock Shading (A) and Realistic Shading (B),
color pencil and ink on Stonehenge paper.

student's first attempt at hooking a flower. Each flower has How to Hook instructions and a primitive approach is described there if it is appropriate for that particular plant.

Mock Shading

Mock shading is a step up from primitive shading. A flower or leaf is shaded with a limited number of values, commonly three to six as in primitive shading, but the values are placed side by side within each petal. The actual direction in which the petal or leaf grows is often neglected in this simple technique.

Notice the difference between mock and realistic shading in the illustration. Instead of following the petals' natural tendency to curve downward, in mock shading the direction of the hooking is horizontal. In fine shading the direction of one's hooking always follows the growth of the plant. Illustration (A) is an example of mock shading; (B) is an example of fine shading.

Fine Shading or Painting with Wool

Fine shading will yield the most realistic flower. Think of yourself as a painter with a palette of wool strips. The technique to master is called *fingering*. Fingering can be compared to the long and short stitch in needlepoint, where the various values meet and slide between each other, like fingers meshing together.

The illustration shows that sometimes values meet tip to tip, while other times they fall between the lines. The lights and darks in the petal should flow seamlessly together. For this to happen, you should never start or stop the next value in the same spot where you ended the preceding one. Values should mix and should never look stripey. The illustration shows the right way to finger (A) and wrong way (B). Three different values are shown in colors.

When you're working with fine shading, remember the following important points:

- Always hook the lightest petal first. In a rose, for instance, the lightest petals are usually on the outside. Proceed to the next lightest, and so forth, until you reach the darkest recesses of the flower.
- Decide how many values to place in each petal. A common number would be two or three, but if you are using an eight- or ten-value gradation, three to five values in each petal are not

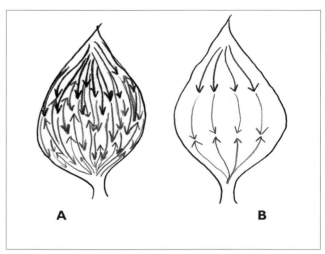

Fingering: Right (A) and Wrong (B),
color pencil and ink on Stonehenge paper.

unusual. The level of detail and realism is up to you.

- As you finger, maintain a curved line. Petals are not straight; hooking straight rows on a curved petal will flatten the illusion of a curved, realistic petal.
- Shade a flower with any cut, but be sure your flower is the appropriate size for that cut. A flower that is 16" wide can be hooked with a #8 cut on linen, but render the same flower with a #3 or #4 cut, and you will end up hooking the endless petal—one that takes a long, long time to fill.
- Every petal joins with the stem.
- Place the darkest values near the center unless there has been a decision to reverse them.
- Consider the unique aspects of each flower in your rug. Lighter backgrounds require that the darker value be placed on the outside edge of the petal, while dark backgrounds require just the opposite.
- Start on the left side of the petal, and establish the curve. Do the same on the right side. Work back and forth toward the interior of the petal, always keeping its curvature in mind. There are a few exceptions to this rule, and they are mentioned in the sections on individual flowers.
- *Do not skip values* within a petal's interior. If you skip from a tint to a medium value without the light colors in between, you will lose the seamless flow of color.
- *Do skip values* between petals. A very dark value is often required to separate petals. This type of skip is acceptable. If the entire petal is finished and the petals do not appear separated, squeeze a few dark loops between the petals. Strong contrast is always needed between petals or else the flower

will lack depth and its form will be lost. Choosing one value darker may be sufficient to achieve the proper separation between blossoms. Occasionally you may need to skip two or three values.

➤ Keep track of the value you are working with. It is easy to become distracted by the television or the telephone. Place your hook on top of the value you used last. This simple reminder will make it easy to pick up where you ended.

➤ Keep the values separated. For instance, fold a simple brown paper bag accordion style to form wells into which you can place the woolen strips. Some rug hookers use cups for this purpose. You'll also find many helpful products on the market.

➤ If your strips become mixed up and it is difficult to see which one is light and which is darker, twist the two strips together to make it easier to distinguish the values.

➤ Stay inside the lines. Wool tends to expand, and remember that flowers are delicate.

Close-Ups: Hooking with ½" strips and Shaded Wide Cuts (#6 to #8)

Large wall hangings or rugs 36" and larger that portray oversized flowers are called close-ups. When hooking the design, only a small part of the whole picture can be seen. This form of rug hooking combines the shading of fine-cut rugs with the speed of hooking wide cuts. The rugs are made with ½"-wide, hand-ripped wool in six to eight values. A large rug measuring 50" by 50" can be completed in three to four weeks. Shaded wide cuts with strips from #6 to 8 are fast to hook. Both close-ups and shaded wide cuts yield dramatic floral fiber art.

The principles used to create a finely shaded flower with these wider cuts are the same as those with the smaller cuts, with some exceptions:

➤ Always use the best quality wool when hand-ripping strips because lesser quality fabrics are difficult to rip and tend to fray.

➤ Use a medium to coarse hook imbedded in a large handle. A large handle is easier to grip with the entire fist and encourages arm pulling instead of wrist action.

➤ Oversized frames (larger than 16" square) are terrific but unnecessary. Avoid lap hoops; instead, use a simple frame on a stand.

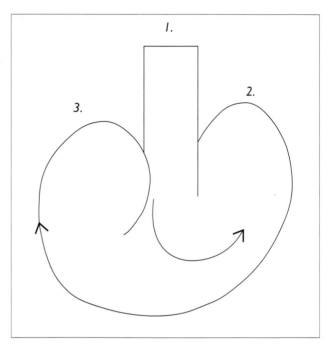

Hiding Tails, *ink on paper.*

➤ Use a large pattern (greater than 30" wide and long) when working with ripped strips. The larger the strip, the larger your pattern and foundation should be.

Finger the values in these rugs just as you would with a narrow cut. The process of placing values between values with wide cuts takes more muscle, but you can do it. For small spaces, rip or cut the wool a bit narrower.

When hooking a wide strip, the fabric wants to curl under. Pull the strip higher so that the loop opens up fully, then adjust it back down to the height of the other loops. Working in this way allows the wool to cover more foundation, provides a smoother appearance, and is an efficient use of fabric.

For a smoother appearance on the surface, hide the tails. In the illustration, pull up the tail at #1. Go back a space to pull up a loop at #2. Finally move forward to place another loop at #3. The tail is captured between two loops.

Characteristics of a Petal

Some flowers can be identified by their petals even when those petals are separated from the main flower. Think of a bearded tulip or a giant iris. The veining and ruffled edges of these flowers' petals are dead giveaways as to the species. When these features are distinguishing characteristics, you need to hook them prominently in the design; otherwise, you may fail to capture the most recognizable aspect of the flower.

Petal Veins

In some flowers, prominent petal veins are their distinguishing characteristic. In this case, make every effort to enhance the veins. If the veins are so light that hooking them will not make a difference in the character of the plant, omit the veins and focus on another aspect of the flower.

Selecting a value for the veins is a challenge and often requires trial and error. Start one value darker than the petal. Use your judgment as you experiment; stand back from the rug and squint your eyes for a different perspective.

Control the prominence of the vein by cutting the strip either finer or wider than the cut of the actual petal.

Petal Rolls

Petal rolls occur at the outside edge of a petal. Hook them in lighter values. Notice in the illustration that the darkest shadow underneath the roll is carried slightly past the place where the roll ends. This end point is indicated with an X. This small detail makes the roll visually happen. A similar approach is used for leaf turnovers.

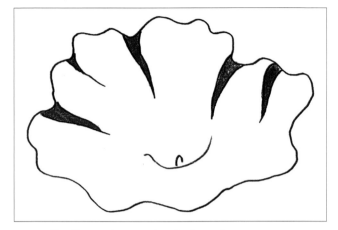

Ruffles, *color pencil and ink on Canson paper.*

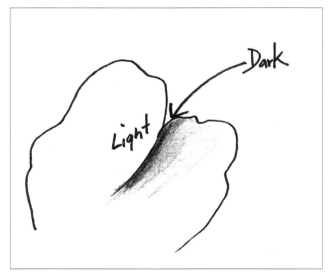

Creases, *color pencil and ink on Canson paper.*

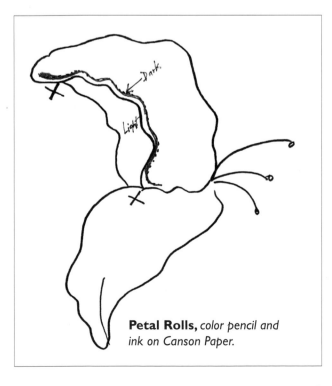

Petal Rolls, *color pencil and ink on Canson Paper.*

Ruffled Edges and Creases

Each ruffle and fold moves from direct sun into shade and shadow many times within each petal. They are easiest to hook in a large flower where you have adequate space. In certain flowers, such as morning glories, folds cannot be overlooked or omitted. When the edge of a petal dips or folds inward, your design should show a shadow and a possible ruffle.

Think of the ruffle as a triangle, with the wide part of the triangle at the edge of the flower, and the narrow point leading into the petal. Make each ruffle a little different in length and width.

A crease is light on one side and dark on the other.

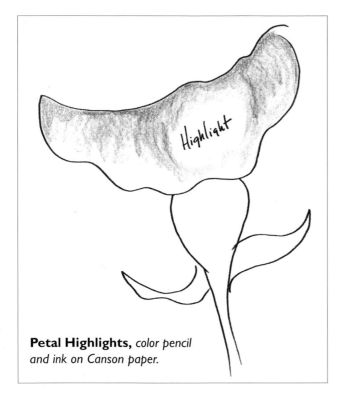

Petal Highlights, *color pencil and ink on Canson paper.*

Petal Highlights

Every rounded object has a highlight. Place the highlight off-center rather than in the middle. Always remember to hook the highlight in the lightest tint. Next to it, hook the light value completely around the highlight. Then hook the medium-light value until you have the entire area shaded.

Flower Centers

Every flower has a unique center. Detailed instructions and illustrations for hooking each are included in this book. Try these great techniques when you hook a flower center on a wall hanging.

    ❧ Raise the loops of the flower's center higher than the normal loops and leave them like this. This technique is called *loop shagging*.

    ❧ Raise the loops of the flower's center higher than normal and fill every hole. Cut all the loops in the center, and shape the wool so the sides slope downward from the top. This technique is called *sculpting*.

    ❧ Raise a section of the center higher than normal and an adjoining section lower. This technique is called *high–low hooking*. A good place to try it is in the center of a sunflower.

    ❧ Add beads for a wonderful and unique center.

    ❧ Use the technique called *pixelating* to create the effect of little seeds. In this technique, twist the wool in your fingers before bringing it to the surface. It is like creating a French knot with wool.

Swatches and Cross-Swatching

Swatches play a key role in portraying flowers. A swatch is a gradation. This transition of lighter to darker values may include as few as three (light, medium, and dark) or as many as eight or more values of a particular color. The greater the number of values in a swatch, the greater the detail afforded the artist in rendering a realistic flower.

Cross-swatching is done when two different colored swatches are paired together in the same flower, often within the same petal. Matching the value and color temperature is the key to success. Color temperature means selecting colors sitting side by side on the color clock. Good combinations would therefore include blue and purple, purple and pink, yellow and orange, or white and yellow.

Just because the values on a swatch fall in exactly the same place does not necessarily mean they can be cross-swatched. For example, sometimes Value 1 in a blue swatch matches Value 3 in a purple swatch. Match values using your eyes regardless of where they fall in the gradation.

Cross-swatching is spectacular in a floral rug because it is the perfect way to carry the color evenly across the design. Artists use it to expand the selection of color and value in a complicated flower like an iris or a chrysanthemum. It is truly the ultimate technique in painting with wool.

Directional Hooking

Hooking directions within individual petals varies from flower to flower, depending on the basic petal form. Each flower provides directional clues; just look at the lines in the petal veins. Sometimes the direction is very obvious, while other times the actual flower or a reference photo has to be closely studied. In this book, each flower is accompanied by a drawing with arrows that indicate hooking direction.

One of the most confusing aspects of hooking a flower is how to direct the line of hooking when one petal lies on top of another. When this happens, imagine the petals that lie underneath. Although you cannot see them, the lower petals will affect the directional hooking of the petals on top. The illustration uses dotted red lines to indicate the invisible petal underneath. The solid arrows point out the correct line of hooking.

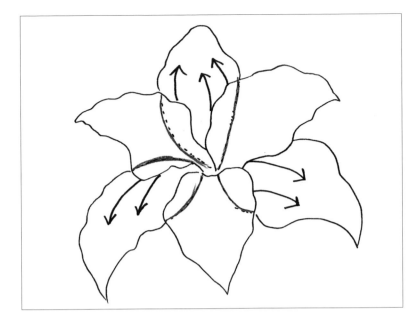

Directional Hooking: *Overlapping Petals.*

Directional Hooking: *Backgrounds.*

ORDER OF HOOKING

Always start with the petal that is fully visible and work back into the flower. In the illustrations, the order of hooking is indicated by numbers. Where the same number appears more than once, hook all of the petals in that group before moving to the next one.

In most floral rugs, the background is hooked in swirling lines. One row of the background fabric is hooked around each flower and leaf. This row is termed a *holding line*, shown in red. The pattern hooked out from this holding line resembles a jigsaw puzzle. Flowers have curves and movement, so it is natural to surround them with curved lines. ☉

CHAPTER FOUR

Color and Materials

"I perhaps owe having become a painter to flowers."—Claude Monet

Flower Color

Selecting colors for a floral rug is the first challenge. Almost every flower is available in a wide range of colors. Tulips, for instance, come in at least 100 different hues and color combinations. Knowing where to start in selecting a color for a particular flower is the first decision.

Many tools can guide you. Get your name on the mailing list of a few good seed and bulb catalogs. Several are listed in the resource section. The Internet is often overlooked as a resource. Visit *www.flowers.vg* for a quick way to see the many color possibilities for a particular flower. Use Google and search under "tulip images" for a large number of color choices.

Colors are listed for each flower featured in this book. In some cases there is only a short list. This list may grow in the future as new varieties are being developed every day.

Challenging Color Matches

Some flower colors are harder than others to replicate in a hooked rug. Let's take a look at the top two most difficult: white and yellow.

White Flowers

A white flower is defined only by its shadows or by the dark background that supports it. Counterintuitively, any white object, including a white flower, is seventy-five percent color and only twenty-five percent pure white. The larger the flower's surface is, the greater the percentage of pure white within it. The area where the sun shines and creates a highlight is the best location for white. A small amount of yellow can enhance this highlight.

The darkest values are placed in the shadows between petals. The dark values of a white flower may be comparable to only light or medium values for another flower. Tints of pink, blue, and lavender can be perfect. Gray is often used instead of pastels, but it has a tendency to yield a washed-out appearance. Instead, mix a small amount of gray in with the brighter pastels.

LEBEL WHITES

Nancy MacLennan hooked the rug, *Lebel*, as a white flower challenge for herself and a group of teachers. She used three formulas from Prisms #2 to dye ten values for the flowers. Her first value was dyed over white wool, the remaining values over natural.

Nancy's leaves were dyed with Prisms #17 B (Forest) over mint wool and Prisms #12 A (Lime) over natural wool.

Prism Red Onion #30
⅛ tsp. Fuchsia #349 (PC)
⅛ tsp. Yellow #119 (PC)
1/32 tsp. Turquoise #478 (PC)

Prism Milkweed #36
⅛ tsp. Yellow #119 (PC)
1/32 tsp. Fuchsia #349 (PC)
1/64 tsp. Turquoise #478 (PC)

Prism Storm #29
1/16 tsp. Turquoise #478 (PC)
⅛ tsp. Fuchsia #349 (PC)
⅛ tsp. Yellow #119 (PC)

Lebel, *32" x 38", #3-cut wool on burlap.*
Designed by Jane McGown Flynn and hooked by Nancy MacLennan, Binghamton, New York, 1994. NANCY MACLENNAN

To get a better idea of how the whites work, take a photograph of the finished flower. Areas where the shadows between petals need to be deeper in value will show up immediately because the flower will lack depth in a two-dimensional photo. It may be necessary to add darker values between petals.

Yellow Flowers

The challenge of a yellow flower is twofold. The values in a yellow gradation are difficult to see, especially in the lightest and the darkest values. Utilizing two compatible swatches in a yellow flower, such as yellow and orange or yellow and white, can expand color and value choices and makes hooking these flowers easier.

In addition, selecting the colors and values to be used within the shadows is a challenge. Finding the correct value may require some trial and error. A good starting place is the opposite of yellow, which is lavender or purple. Or use either greens or oranges in the dark recesses of the flower. Marian Hall did a great job in selecting her shadows in *Amelia's Daffodil*. (See below.) Marion says she spent one day dyeing twenty-five to thirty shades of golds and yellows. The colors between the petals are shades of greenish gold; some have a gray cast. The forward facing petal in the center is outlined with purple to make it stand out.

Amelia's Daffodil, *detail.*
See full rug on page 110.

Here is a hypothetical example of how to think through a color plan. In this example, the artist made decisions early and had a roadmap.

This hypothetical plan selected the first family, which is in the hours noon through 4 o'clock and the colors yellow, yellow-green, green, blue-green, and blue. The poison (distant cousin) is opposite green, the third color in the family. In this case, the poison is red or pink. The common background choices for Family #1 are green, blue-green, and blue. Yellow and yellow-green would be more challenging background choices. Old ivory makes a gorgeous pale yellowish background, and a dark sage green is a wonderful member of the yellow-greens; however, they are not commonly chosen as background colors for Family #1.

1. The artist selects a dark navy background. Other potential choices might have been an antique green, a dark blue such an indigo blue, or a dark turquoise.
2. The leading lady is a yellow hibiscus with a pink center. Pink is the poison.
3. The foliage is the supporting cast and is hooked with light blues, yellow-greens, blue-greens, and gray-greens. Watch the value of the leaves to be sure they show up against the dark background.
4. The artist carries the leading lady's color into some of the veins along with some of the pink poison. A spot dye containing gold and pink tones and a little blue would be excellent for the veins. Always work floral colors into the leaves.

Color Planning

Color planning should never be rushed. Mistakes happen when a rug hooker uses leftover materials without careful thought about how each component of the rug—whether flowers, background, or border—will come together to create a unified whole. The following color planning steps will yield a successful outcome.

Basic Color Planning Steps

1. Choose the value of the background. Will it be light or dark?
2. Choose the background color.

Color Clock, *computer graphic. Designed by Marc Senger, Quincy, Massachusetts, 2009.*

3. Decide on the rug's focal point. Which single flower or group deserves special attention?

4. Then choose a color for that flower or grouping. Think of this focal point as your leading lady. Everything else in the rug is less important in terms of color and contrast.

5. Evaluate the other flowers and choose two additional colors to be supporting actors. Make sure each flower stands out against the background.

6. Choose a poison. The poison is used in small amounts to add an extra spark to the rug. It is the equivalent of the renowned actor playing the cameo role. The best choice is often found on the color wheel opposite that of the leading lady.

7. Pay attention to the foliage. Choose a variety of greens, but hook the veins in a flower color that is *not* green. (See Chapter 6 for a full explanation.)

Color Limitation

Color limitation is the secret to good color planning! Most rug hookers use too many colors. Instead, it is better to repeat colors in the wide variety of textures and dyed materials that are available.

Think of the color wheel as a clock and divide the clock into twelve families. Each family represents four hours of time on the clock and includes five colors. For instance, the color family starting at 12:00 includes yellow, yellow-green, green, blue-green, and blue (the

hours following 12:00, 1:00, 2:00, 3:00, and 4:00). Each family also includes a poison, which is the distant cousin. When an artist chooses a family, he or she is automatically restricting the number of color choices.

More than five colors in a single rug are too many. The best rugs repeat colors rather than adding colors. Neutrals such as black, tan, and off-white are safe to include in any family. Each family can represent either bright or primitive colors. Primitive colors are grayish versions of a pure color.

Information on how to order Jane's Color Clock Workbook is available in the Resource pages.

Color Balance

Plan your color placement and write the colors on the backing to avoid color imbalances. Bright colors, whites, and your leading lady are particularly crucial here and should be spread as evenly as possible across the rug's surface. Carrying bits of color from one flower to the next and into the veins balances the colors in your rug.

Cross-swatching is another way to ensure color balance. Mixing the colors of two swatches together in one flower expands your options without adding colors that do not fit. In the leaf veins, choose a color that is not green. Reach for a darker hue: spot dyes, plaids, and over-dyed tweeds are great choices.

Check your progress on balancing the colors by squinting or viewing the rug from a distance. Use a

Wild Rose Scroll, *24" x 36", #4- and 5-cut wool on cotton warp cloth. Designed by House of Price and hooked by Ingrid Hieronimus, Petersburg, Ontario, Canada, 2010.* INGRID HIERONIMUS

demagnifying glass (the lens used to create the peep holes in front doors—available at home improvement stores) to see your rug from a different perspective. Or take a photograph of your rug as you are working on it. Photographs often reveal things you don't notice when you look directly at your work.

Backgrounds

The background is the foundation of the rug. I cannot emphasize this point enough: choose your background first. Every other color in the rug depends on this choice, so make the decision and stick with it.

Dark value backgrounds are more dramatic than light ones because they create a greater value contrast among the flowers, foliage, and background. Medium value backgrounds are tricky to work with because motifs often disappear. The easiest backgrounds to work with are those on which the largest number of colors ride well—these are often neutrals and cool colors.

Whenever you put a background's opposite (complementary color) on its surface, there is harmony—for instance, purple on top of old ivory (light yellow) or peach on top of dark blue. Always do something to the background fabric, such as simmer out color, add a bit of another color, or tone it down. Never use the fabric

straight out of the Goodwill bag or straight off of the bolt.

Here is my list of common backgrounds arranged by difficulty, with comments on their use.

Easy Light Backgrounds

Sand, oatmeal, and old ivory. Each of these light neutrals will support any flower color.

Easy Dark Backgrounds

Dark blues such as indigo and navy support almost any color and are safe background choices.

Antique black is my favorite dark green. I include a recipe for this color on page 25.

Blue-green is another easy background. Jane's Green (*page 25*) works well.

Difficult Light Backgrounds

Taupe appears neutral but as a background it leans toward violet. Certain colors such as oranges and bright yellow-greens will go to war with taupe. On the other hand, red-violets or dark purples agree with it.

Light greens are challenging because foliage will compete. If you choose a light green, eliminate the light values on the edges of your green leaves.

Difficult Dark Backgrounds

Red is a difficult color for a background. The best choice is a burgundy red, which contains blue. If you have lots of plain red from the resale shops, first over dye it with blue, green, or black to soften it and gray it down. Certain Navajo rugs contain bright reds, but these are the exception.

Additionally, certain shades of lavender, orange, blue-violet, and yellow-green will fight with a red background. On the other hand, whites, pinks, and yellows are almost always beautiful against a red background.

Ingrid Hieronimus hooked *Wild Rose Scroll* on a red background. An additional challenge in her piece was the red scrolls. Ingrid chose Multiple Fusion Spot #20 dyed as a solid color over Dorr Natural wool for the background color.

Multiple Fusion Spot #20
1/16 tsp. Black #672 (PC)
1/4 tsp. Navy #413 (PC)
1/4 tsp. Bright Red #351 (PC)
1/2 tsp. Sun Yellow #119 (PC)

A brown background deadens a rug. To avoid this near catastrophe, choose a brown with red or gold highlights.

Eggplant is a dark black-violet and can be a gorgeous background with whites, yellows, pinks, and red-violet. Be careful when pairing it with orange and yellow-orange unless these colors are used in small amounts as a poison. Blue, gray, and olive greens ride well on eggplant.

A dark turquoise background supports peach, salmon, and pink flowers beautifully. Yellow, gold, and lighter shades of blue-green are beautiful when paired with teal.

Hard-to-Manage Mid-Value Backgrounds

Even experienced rug hookers can walk into this danger zone and come out limping.

Blue is the #1 example of failed mid-value backgrounds. Both dark and light values can be lost against it. Plan the entire rug out carefully before ever picking up a hook.

Tan is a common background because it abounds in resale shops. Over dye the fabric before using it; preferably turn it into a darker value.

Gold as a background can steal attention away from the design. The same is true of other warm background colors.

Unusual Background Choices

Spot dyes can be used for a background, but be careful. Like warm colors, spot dyes can steal the show by being too busy and detracting from your flowers. Moreover, because spot dyes contain more than one color, they can add too much color to your rug. Remember that the best rugs practice color limitation.

Mixing two values to create shapes in the background creates the illusion of negative space. It creates a sense of mystery in both backgrounds and borders, as seen in the close up of *Botanical Fantasy (page 21)*. The effect is terrific as long as it is subtle and does not take attention away from the floral details.

Dip-dyed backgrounds are often used to create the painterly effect of either a dark or a light value moving outward from the floral detail to the rug's edge. Sometimes the background is hooked in an almost fanlike fashion from the inside edge to the outside edge. An example of this is Marian Hall's daffodil rug *(page 110)*.

A *noodle background* is a technique that works best with a single flower. Elissa Crouch used this approach in *Self Discovery*. The flower is hooked in red-violets, reds, and purples. She chose blues, greens, and blue-greens for the background. These three background colors sit shoulder-to-shoulder on the color clock. Reaching for colors that are closely related is key when utilizing this technique.

In Elissa's rug, every strip of wool came out of a scrap bag filled with cut noodles! She included all cuts from #3 to #8. While planning, she created three piles from her cool colors and divided them into light, medium, and dark piles. The piles included spots, tweeds, and abrashed pieces in all three background colors.

To complete a noodle background, first hook all the shapes around the flower with a selection of blue, blue-green, and green strips in the lightest values. Second, surround the light shapes with the medium values. Finally, surround the medium values with the darkest values, which hug the flower and show it off.

A noodle background may look easy, but it takes planning. Once the values are divided, you can let yourself go and have some fun. You'll find this technique is a great way to use up your leftovers.

Sweet Pea, border detail.
See full rug on page 70.

Self Discovery (border detail), 24" x 20", #3- and 4-cut wool on linen.
Designed by Jane Halliwell Green and hooked by Elissa Crouch, Cambridge, Maryland, 2011.

Borders

Consider these important facts before you choose a border for your rug:

⚘ Never let a border steal the show. Borders should never be more important than the center of a rug.

⚘ A border that is too bright will grab the viewer's eye and cause him or her to look away from the flowers.

⚘ Flowers within a border also have the potential to steal the show!

⚘ A border must always repeat colors from the interior of the rug. For a floor rug, choose the darker colors because they recede and do a better job of anchoring the rug to the floor.

⚘ Consider a single line of flower color to separate the border from the interior of the piece. Sometimes the leading lady or poison is a good choice.

⚘ Just because a border is drawn on a preprinted pattern does not mean you have to include it.

Botanical Fantasy, *border detail. See full rug on page 23.*

⁓ Borders do not have to be exactly the same width on all sides. This is especially true for wall hangings. Floor rugs traditionally have even borders with the idea that they should be seen equally from four sides. A more artistic approach is to vary the width.

Broken Borders

In a broken border the flowers and foliage change color when they cross a border. In *Botanical Fantasy,* interior color becomes monochromatic as the flower crosses over. Sometimes this change occurs in the middle of a flower

and leaf. Or consider the reverse: a monochromatic color scheme in the center transitions to color in the border.

At one point in *Botanical Fantasy,* the border was broken with color, just below the large flower, which is the focal point of the piece. The artist used this technique to bring the viewer into the picture.

Noodle Borders

The noodle background mentioned earlier can also be used for a border. My color planning scheme in *Sweet Pea* was to hook the border in color Family #11, which

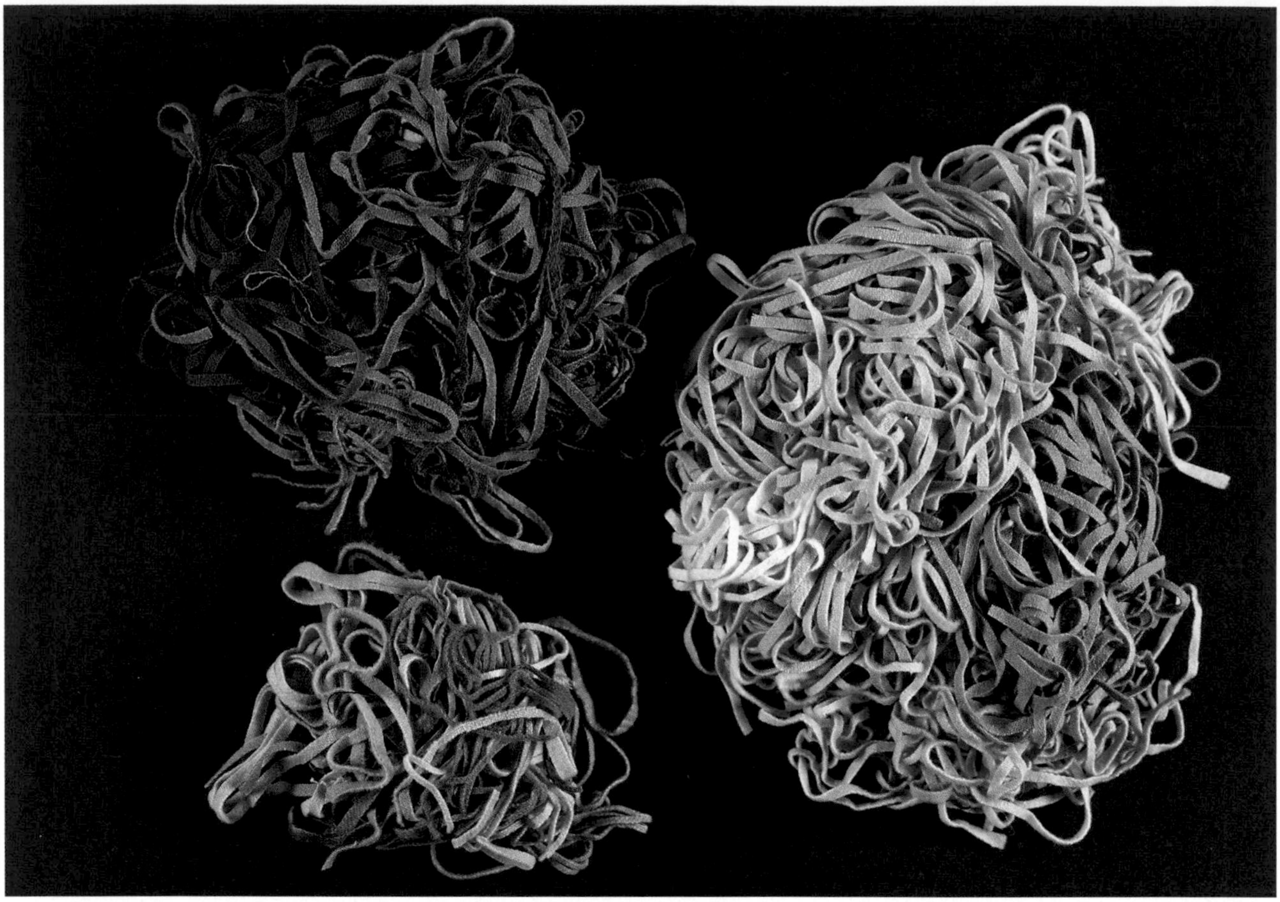

Strips of wool in Family #11, separated by value, to be used in a noodle background.

consists of orange, yellow-orange, yellow, yellow-green, and green; and the flower in purple (a distant cousin to Family #11). With my lightest noodles, I created circles, spirals, and squiggles in the border without a drawing as I hooked intuitively. I followed these light noodles with the medium values and then the darks. I placed a dark line of purple inside the border to separate the inside from outside and to carry the color out. The interior background is sand.

Scrolls

Older floral rugs often have scrolls at the edge of the rug, which have the primary function of framing hooked flowers. Scrolls must always repeat colors from the center of the rug. It is a major mistake to invent a new palette of color for the scroll or to make the scroll the focal point of the design.

Materials

Hooking a family heirloom does not happen quickly; therefore, it is only reasonable to invest in the best materials. Use 100% flannel-weight wool for a floor rug. Be careful of fabrics containing as little as 20% man-made fibers. The greater the percent of man-made acrylic fibers, the more difficult the fabric is to cut and hook.

Never put a piece of as-is wool into your work without simmering color out, adding color, or mottling it in some way in the dye pot. (The exception to this rule is a plaid that might work without the need for trip to the dye pot.) Your alteration can be as simple as simmering out color or spotting it with black. Carefully read the chapter on dyeing to learn how to create the best colors using the best materials. If you are a new rug hooker, buy materials from your teacher or an online provider until you have taken a dye class.

Each flower in this book is accompanied by a suggestion regarding the best materials to use. Some of the simple small flowers can be hooked with a spot dye; however, the majority of the flowers will require 4- to 8-value swatches or dip dyes. Keep in mind that mixing a swatch with a dip dye is always an option.

Tweeds are great materials for stems and flower centers. Use plaids to outline primitive flowers and leaves and to accent the border. They are great additions to an antique black background.

Remember to take time to color plan and choose that important background color first!

Botanical Fantasy, *32" x 47", #3- and 4-cut wool on cotton warp cloth.*
Designed and hooked by Jane Halliwell Green, Edgewater, Maryland, 2008.

CHAPTER FIVE

Dyeing for Flowers

"Be like the flower, turn your faces to the sun."—Kahlil Gibran

Most addicted rug hookers will seek out the dye pot and discover that nothing is better than creating their own colors. Dyeing wool is as easy and as simple as following a recipe. Locate a teacher who offers dye classes or pick up a book on basic dyeing.

BEFORE YOU GET STARTED. . .

- Write everything down so you can duplicate any fabric color you create.
- Stay off the telephone. Dyeing wool demands your full concentration.
- If you are working in your kitchen, lay down plastic and keep your dyeing supplies separate from your cooking utensils. Keep all food away from the area where you are working.
- Wear gloves and a face mask when you are measuring dyes.
- Soak the wool ahead of time in a wetting agent.
- Remember, never boil wool; instead, simmer it. Boiling will felt the fabric, making it unsuitable for rug hooking.

Dyeing Backgrounds

Keep backgrounds simple. If the fabric is too busy then the background will steal the show.

Abrashed Backgrounds

A good background is something called an *abrashed background*, a background with variations of color resulting from differences in wools or dyes. An abrash is created by pouring dye directly on the wool, creating subtle shading differences. I call it "pour and push," because a bit is poured directly on the wool, and then the wool is gently pushed under the water. Turn the wool and keep pouring

Letters appear after each dye listed in this book. (PC) indicates Pro Chemical dyes, (C) stands for Cushing, and (MC) is Majic Carpet dyes. See Resources on page 134 for purchasing information.

SIMPLE SUPPLIES

- One set of regular kitchen measuring spoons
- Turkey roaster, 10" x 15" is best
- Heavy rubber gloves and lighter latex gloves
- Large soup pot, at least 2 quarts
- Three or four 2-cup measuring cups
- Tongs
- 1" flat watercolor brush, for casseroles only
- Paper towels
- Dye spoons (Buy an entire set of spoons for 1/4 tsp., 1/8 tsp., 1/16 tsp., 1/32 tsp., 1/64 tsp., and 1/128 tsp.)
- Wetting agents, such as Synthropol, Jet Dry, and liquid detergent
- White vinegar or citric acid crystals
- 16 oz. canning jars (Buy good quality jars, such as Mason jars; mayonnaise jars break easily.)
- Microwave oven
- Flannel-weight wool
- Dyes: I use three: Pro Chemical, Cushing, and Majic Carpet. If you are new to dyeing, start with Pro Chemical. Purchase their starter kit and basic dye book, *Primary Fusion: A Guide to Dyeing with Only Three Primary Colors Using Pro Chemical Dyes*, by Ingrid Hieronimus.
- Wooden spoons

*Wool for the antique black background of **Angels Among Us**. See the full rug on page 105.*

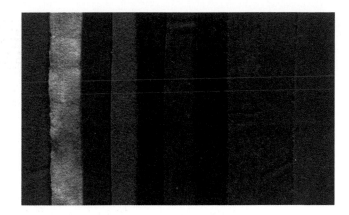

and pushing until you have abrashed quite a bit of the fabric. Add either white vinegar or citric acid crystals as the last step. When the water in the pot is clear, wash and dry the fabric.

Here are four of my favorite treatments:

❧ Dissolve ¹/₄ tsp. Black #672 (PC) in 1 cup of hot water. Pour directly over 1 yd. of dark green, navy blue, or eggplant wool.

❧ Dissolve ¹/₄ tsp. of Violet #818 (PC) over 1 yd. of navy or dark blue wool.

❧ Dissolve ¹/₄ tsp. of Old Ivory (C) over 1 yd. of natural wool. This makes a beautiful light background.

❧ Dissolve ¹/₄ tsp. Taupe (C) over 1 yd. of natural wool for a good neutral background that leans toward violet.

Antique Black

Antique black is a beautiful background for a floral rug. It is very dark, and since it is created from a variety of materials, it creates a sense of movement around flowers without detracting from them. The background of *Angels Among Us* illustrates this clearly.

Start by collecting fabrics. Antique black requires medium dark to dark fabrics such as black, gray, greens of all types, blues, checks, plaids, and purple. This is a good opportunity to use up the garish materials you found in the resale shops—remember to always look for 100% flannel-weight wool for the best results. This background is created with scraps of all sizes. In rug hooking we call this technique "marrying our colors."

1. Presoak your materials.
2. Add all of the fabrics plus ¹/₄ cup of liquid detergent to the pot, and simmer for 15 to 30 minutes. The detergent helps force color out of the fabrics, making them bleed out into the water and intermingle.
3. When the pot is murky, add a generous ½ cup of white vinegar. Vinegar is the mordant and will force the color back into the wool.
4. Cook another 15 minutes and let the pot cool down until the water is cold.
5. Wash and dry the wool. If the value of the wool seems too light after it is dry, repeat the process with ¹/₄ teaspoon of Black #672 (PC) dissolved in 1 cup of hot water.

6. Cut the fabric strips, and hook them into your rug at random. Nothing should jump out; all should blend beautifully.
7. Antique black may leave lint on your work. To avoid this, hook the flowers first and then cover them with a towel while you hook the background.

JANE'S GREEN

This dark blue-green spot dye is a beautiful background.

1. Scrunch light green wool in the turkey roaster.
2. Dissolve 1 tsp. of #728 Green (PC) in 1 cup of hot water.
3. Dissolve 1 tsp. of Myrtle Green (C) in 1 cup of hot water.
4. Randomly spot the presoaked wool with the two dyes.
5. Pour ¹/₁₆ tsp. of #672 Black (PC) plus ½ cup of white vinegar over the entire piece of fabric.
6. Add lots of water and simmer for 20 to 30 minutes.

Red Backgrounds

Most wool collectors end up with barrels of red. When red is commercially dyed, it bleeds profusely, so some of the color must be removed and reset. Even after this process, color fastness cannot be guaranteed.

1. Presoak the red wool.
2. Simmer it with ¹/₂ cup of liquid detergent. Pour off the first pot of water, and repeat the process with more detergent.
3. Add ¹/₄ tsp. of blue #425 (PC) or ¹/₄ tsp. of Black #672 (PC) to tone down the red.
4. Simmer at least 20 minutes before adding white vinegar or citric acid crystals. Continue cooking until the color in the pot clears. Let the wool remain in the pot until the water is cold.

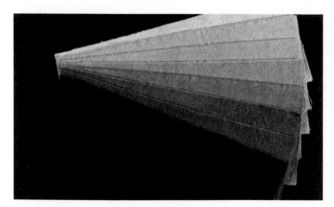

Single color swatch, *dyed on natural wool.*

Transitional swatch, *dyed on natural wool.*

Swatches

Hooking realistic flowers requires a great number of values. The rug hookers' answer to finding those values is a *swatch*. A swatch is wool that is dyed in several values of color ranging from light to dark. The directions that follow are based on a 6-value swatch. A swatch is considered a straight gradation when the values are created using only one color. A transitional swatch means the values were created using two colors.

Two methods are used to dye swatches: open pan and jar dyeing. Unless you need to dye a large quantity of wool, a good place to begin is with the jars.

Jar Dyeing: One-Color Straight Gradation

1. Gather six 16-ounce Mason jars.
2. Soak 6 pieces of flannel-weight wool measuring 6" x 12".
3. Fill the turkey roaster $1/3$ to $1/2$ full with water.
4. Fill the Mason jars halfway full with water, and place them in the turkey roaster. Six jars should fit in one turkey roaster.
5. Measure the dry dye into 1 cup of hot water. This is your dye formula.
6. Now prepare each jar:
   - Measure $1/2$ tsp. from your dye formula into Jar 1; this is Value 1.
   - Measure $1 1/2$ tsp. into Jar 2; this is Value 2.
   - Measure 1 Tbsp. into Jar 3; this is Value 3.
   - Measure 2 Tbsp. into Jar 4; this is Value 4.
   - Measure 4 Tbsp. into Jar 5; this is Value 5.
   - Measure 8 Tbsp. into Jar 6; this is Value 6.
7. Add a piece of wool to each jar, and stir.
8. Bring the heat up and stir, stir, stir! The more you stir the more evenly the material will be dyed.
9. Wait 15 to 20 minutes until the water in the turkey roaster is at a simmer before adding 1 Tbsp. of vinegar to each jar. Continue to stir. **Note:** Do not add the vinegar too soon or the wool will not thoroughly absorb the dye; your result will be a piece of wool

with a white core. Continue to cook the wool until the water in the jars is clear. In certain formulas, particularly red, the water may not completely clear. This is particularly true with the darkest value.

10. Cool down, and enjoy!

Jar Dyeing: Two-Color Transitional Swatch

In a two-color transitional swatch, the values range from the dark shade of one color to the light shade of another color.

1. Mix two formulas:

   Color #1: Follow the directions given regarding the quantity of water and dye.

   Color #2: Follow the directions given regarding the quantity of water and dye.

2. Set up the 6 jars in the turkey roaster as described in the one-color straight gradation.
3. Place 1 Tbsp. of Color 1 in every jar.
4. Measure your gradation for Color 2 as in the one-color straight gradation described earlier.

Dip Dyes

Unlike a swatch, where each value is limited to separate pieces of wool, a dip dye contains multiple values on one piece of wool. Some flowers, such as tulips and day lilies, are easier to hook using a dip dye. Leaves, especially strap leaves, are especially effective when hooked with a dip dye. If the dipped strip is handled well, the flower almost hooks itself.

The disadvantage of a dip dye is that it is impossible to place six values on a single piece of wool. A dip dye can only hold a light, medium, and dark value. Very dark values have to be dyed separately and used in conjunction with the dipped strips.

- Wear heavy gloves. Your hands get close to the hot water when you are dipping.
- A standard-sized strip is 6" x 18", but you can cut the wool to fit the flower. The formula on the next page is not perfectly precise because we

all hook differently. Hookers who hook tight and low use less wool than those who hook loose and high. Sometimes the measurement is perfect for the outside of the flower but a little long for the inside.

    Formula: Measure the length of the petal and multiply it by your cut. If the petal is 6" long and I am using a #4 cut, that means I would need my wool to be 24" long. If I decided on a #8 cut, the size would be 6 multipied by 8, or 48" long. The wider the cut, the longer the strip will be. Adjust for a loose hooker by adding another 1" or 2", but reduce the size for those who hook tightly. (Yes, I realize I could be quoted out of context on this point!)

One-Color Dip Dye

1. Measure the dye formula, and add ¼ up vinegar to the dye solution. The mordant must be added with the dye so the wool will grab the color. Simmer the wool 20 minutes in additional vinegar or citric acid crystal to set the dye.
2. Fill a turkey roaster or soup pot with water and bring up the heat.
3. Add the formula slowly. Start with ¼ to ½ cup. One cup of formula can dye many strips.
4. Hold the wool in your gloved hand and begin dipping. One piece at a time is easiest, but as you become more dexterous, you can hold two pieces. Keep the wool moving so that straight lines do not form across the fabric. Your goal is a smooth transition from light to dark.
5. After a few minutes, dip even more of the fabric into the pot. The dark end is where you began and now you are creating the middle value.
6. Finally, turn the wool upside-down, and dip the other end in to create the lightest value. Sometimes a quick drop in the dye pot is all you need. Place this wool in a second pot containing the mordant. Place light values and dark values on top of each other, and simmer for about 20 minutes.

Two-Color Dip Dye

1. Prepare two formulas each in a separate cup of hot water with 1 Tbsp. of vinegar.

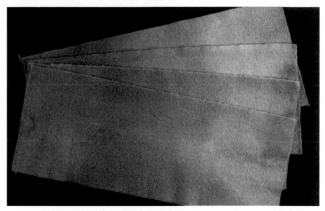

Three-color dip dye, *dyed on natural wool.*

2. Prepare two pots, and bring up the heat.
3. Add your formulas slowly.
4. Dip the first half of the strip into the first pot.
5. Flip to the other side of the strip and dip it into the second color.

    Important: *Always overlap your colors. If you find the colors to be too light, add more formula and repeat the process.*

Casseroles

Fabulous leaves, leaf veins, and tendrils can be created with casserole dyeing. In a casserole, as many as four or five colors can be placed on one strip of wool.

    Use a 10" x 15" turkey roaster pan. Cut the wool to exactly the same size as the pan.

    Have lots of paper towels available.

    Presoak the wool.

    Be prepared to babysit the dye pot. This process is slow.

    Keep the cups in order. It is easy to get confused!

    Some formulas are simple because the colors are closely related, such as blue and purple. Other formulas involving two colors that are opposite each other (green and red, for instance) become gray where they touch.

    If you have leftover dye, do not be tempted to throw it into your casserole. Save it for another time.

1. Dissolve each color in 1 cup of hot water with either vinegar or citric acid crystals. Crystals are preferred because they do not dilute the formula.

2. Scrunch up paper towels into balls, and place them on the sides of the pan where one color might bleed into another. These paper dams will prevent the colors from becoming muddy.

3. Layer the wool in the pan. Wring out each piece before placing it on top of the next. Think of making lasagna: if you add too much tomato sauce the lasagna will be soupy when it comes out of the oven. Only use as much water and dye as you need. Do not let lots of color pool along the sides of the pan.

4. As you layer the wool in the pan, always place the same color on top of the one beneath. If you break this rule, the colors will become muddy.

5. Place each color on the wool, and overlap them by using either your gloved fingers or a watercolor brush.

6. Simmer for a few minutes. You'll hear a sizzle and smell the wool burning. This is when you add a small amount of clear water on the sides. Keep watching the wool and adding a little more water. After about 10 minutes, reach under the wool and flip all of the pieces over. This distributes the heat and ensures the color on the top pieces will be set. After 15 minutes it is safe to add more water. Cook the wool about 25 minutes, and then allow it to cool down. Rinse and dry. The bottom piece will be your darkest.

Spot Dyes

Spot dyes are needed for stems, veins, tendrils, flower centers, and the outlines of primitive florals. Spot dyes are often the fabric of choice in selecting a poison to provide the zing in a rug. The formulas in this section use 1 yard of wool. Cut the formula in half for ½ yard of wool.

1. Scrunch the presoaked wool in a flat turkey roaster.

2. Dissolve each formula in 1 cup of hot water. Some spot dyes require 3 colors; others, 4.

3. Randomly spot the wool, and *do* let the colors overlap.

4. Add water and vinegar under the wool if you want very spotty material or directly on top if you want to mute the colors.

5. Cover the pot and cook the wool on top of the stove for 30 minutes, or cover it with tinfoil and bake at 250° for 45 minutes.

Fry Pot Dyeing

Fry pot dyeing is done in a small fry pot with a basket. Most formulas are three or four color formulas for ¹/₂ yard of wool. This is a slow process. Do this type of dyeing at the same time you are dyeing on the stove or hooking.

1. Dissolve each dye in 1 cup of hot water.

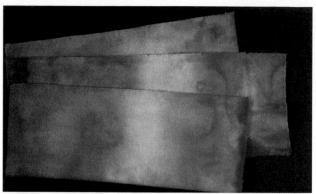

Casserole dyeing, *dyed on natural wool.*

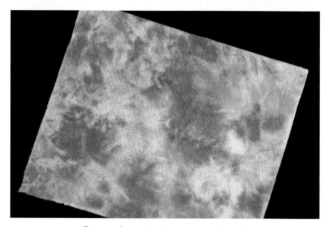

Spot dye, *dyed on natural wool.*

2. Wrap the wool in the basket like a turban.

3. Add the first dye and the wool in the basket to the fry pot. The water will be cold.

4. Raise the heat to a simmer. Once it's hot, add the vinegar or citric acid crystals.

5. Cook for another 10 to 15 minutes, and then turn off the heat. Let the pot cool down.

6. Repeat this procedure with all the other colors. Between each color, rinse the wool and rewind it in the fry basket to expose a new dye to other parts of the fabric. ✺

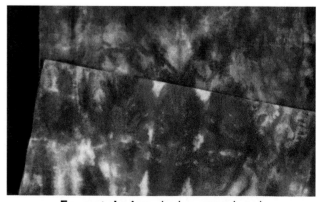

Fry pot dyeing, *dyed on natural wool.*

CHAPTER SIX

Leaves, Stems, and Veins

Autumn, *32" x 51", #3-cut wool on burlap. Designed and hooked by Jeanne Field, Aurora, Ontario, 2000.* ANDREA FIELD

"The earth laughs in flowers."
—Ralph Waldo Emerson

Rendering leaves in fiber can be as challenging as hooking flowers. The foliage surrounds and supports the flowers and carries colors across the design's surface. To hook realistic foliage, you need to eliminate any preconceived idea that leaves must be green or absolutely perfect. Nature doesn't follow this rule of perfection, so why should we? Fall leaves are combinations of red, orange, yellow, gold, green, and purple. Even green itself is a multitude of hues from yellow-green to purple-green. In addition, the back of a leaf may be a different color and value than the front.

When I first started hooking rugs, my teacher asked me to describe the foliage in my backyard. Her thought-provoking question provided an excellent lesson to me—

Autumn, *detail.*

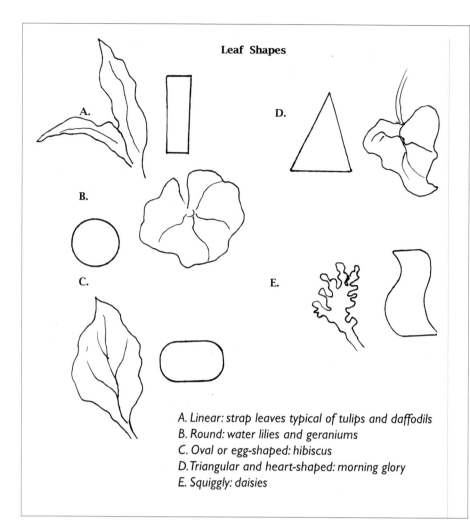

Leaf Shapes

A. Linear: strap leaves typical of tulips and daffodils
B. Round: water lilies and geraniums
C. Oval or egg-shaped: hibiscus
D. Triangular and heart-shaped: morning glory
E. Squiggly: daisies

Leaf Shapes, *color pencil and ink on Stonehenge paper.*

The five primary leaf shapes:
A. Long, narrow leaves typical of the strap leaves of a tulip or daffodil are *linear.*
B. *Round* leaves remind us of lily pads.
C. A hibiscus leaf is oval or egg-shaped.
D. *Triangular* or heart-shaped leaves are found on the morning glory.
E. Daisies are known to have *squiggly* foliage.

The five primary leaf edges:
A. Smooth
B. Wavy
C. Lobed
D. Rough
E. Saw

a student who was intent on using a single piece of green wool for her leaves—by pointing out that nature is multichromatic and that no two leaves are exactly alike.

Jeanne Field proved that she was an expert on the subject of leaves when she created the rug *Autumn.* Jeanne was traveling through the town of Picton, Ontario, during the fall and was inspired by the colorful foliage. She collected 50 leaves, which she pressed between wax paper and then arranged on a piece of drawing paper cut to the size of her rug. She spent all day moving the leaves around on the paper until she liked the design. She then traced around the leaves and hooked a sensational rug.

Foliage is present in an infinite variety of shapes. There are tall strap leaves that twist and turn, tiny ivy leaves, big and boisterous botanical specimens, and short and hairy leaves like those of an African violet. The illustration above depicts five of the more common leaf shapes, though in the dictionary you can find as many as fifty types described. Become familiar with these shapes, the different kinds of leaf edges, and the terms used to describe them.

Let's take a look at some general guidelines for hooking leaves; however, please realize that you'll find variations depending on the characteristics of the individual plant. Detailed instructions will appear in each specific flower chapter.

Color Planning

Larger rugs can support a greater number of foliage colors than smaller rugs. Plan the foliage after selecting the background and flower colors. Lay the leaf colors on top of the background colors and beside the flower colors. Choose light values for leaf edges lying against a dark background and darker values when a light background will be used. These choices will ensure good contrast between the foliage and your backdrop. If you have any doubt about how a leaf will appear against your background, hook a few lines of both fabrics side by side. If an occasional leaf fades a bit into the background, don't worry. Focus on the majority.

Variety is the key. Just because a particular flower has yellow-green leaves is not a reason to eliminate other colors. Strive for a mixture of blue-greens, yellow-greens, and silver gray-greens. Gray-greens are safe because they complement almost any flower color, but be careful not

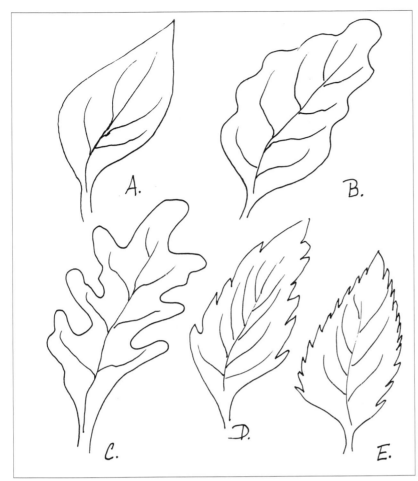

Leaf Edges, *color pencil and ink on Stonehenge paper.*

CHOOSING A VEIN COLOR

Unless you are using fall colors, green veins are unacceptable. Instead, always include the flower color in the veins.

- A spot dye containing many or all of the rug's colors or an over-dyed tweed or plaid that picks up some of the colors in the rug is one choice. Spot dyes create a line that does not look solid.
- Gold and purple, leftover scraps or dye pot mistakes, or darker values stolen from flowers make sensational veins. When in doubt always choose darker values.
- And one caution: Avoid bright colors and light values unless the particular leaf's characteristics require it. For example, cyclamen leaves have distinctive light veins and markings that should be played up.

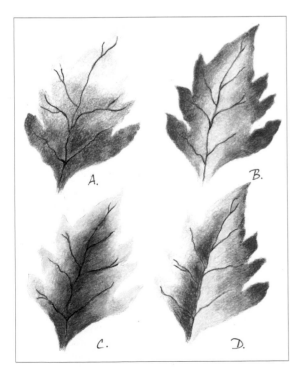

Leaf Shading, *color pencil and ink on Stonehenge paper.*

to overuse them. Yellow, red, orange, and spots of green are great for fall leaves.

Use transitional swatches and casserole dyes to add additional interest to the foliage. Some greens are neutral and look good with any color—often these are the low intensity greens. Bright yellow-greens jump out, so be careful of these.

Most leaves are divided down the center by a central vein called the *mid-rib*. It is not necessary to hook both sides of the mid-rib exactly the same. In fact, it is far better to treat each side differently. In the leaf shading drawing, you can see some of the possibilities. A lack of perfect balance is good!

A. A dark base to a light tip.

B. A light center on both sides of the vein ending with a darker edge.

C. A dark center on both sides of the middle vein ending with light edges.

D. Dark on the left side of the vein finishing with a light edge. Doing the reverse: a light value on the right side of the vein and ending darker at the edge.

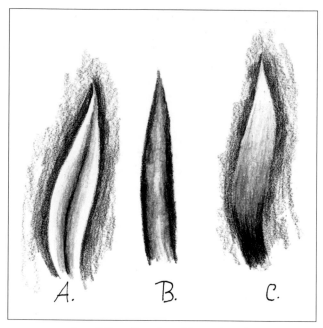

Leaf Shading in a Strap Leaf,
color pencil on Stonehenge paper.

Linear or strap leaves like those found surrounding a tulip will not have a prominent central vein. The shading possibilities are more linear:

A. dark middle and a light edge.

B. A light center finishing with a dark edge.

C. A dark base ending in a light tip.

Hooking Leaves

Creating foliage to frame your flower can be as much fun as hooking the flowers. Let's explore the different styles and parts of the leaves.

Primitive

Outlining is perfect for a primitive leaf. Make it interesting: outline the leaf with a plaid or tweed and fill it in with a solid abrashed color, or outline it with a solid and fill it in with a plaid or tweed. Use outlining to carry the flower colors around the rug. Feel free to omit the veins running outward from the central rib.

Realistic

In a realistic floral, the lines of hooking flow in the same direction as the veins and the growth of the plant. Hook the vein first, and work outward from it. Use the fingering technique, hooking one side of the leaf at a time. In most instances the base of the leaf and the area where the stem meets the flower are darker. Follow the arrows on the illustrations.

Small leaves are easier to hook because they do not need many values. Limit your values to three or less. Sometimes a single spot dye will be sufficient.

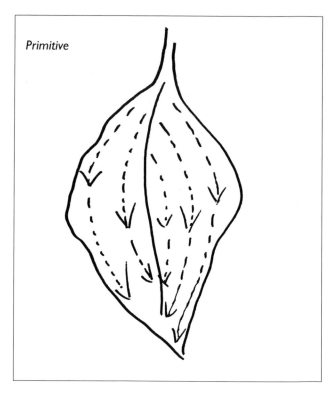

Primitive

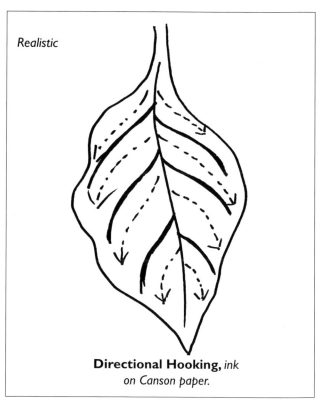

Realistic

Directional Hooking, *ink on Canson paper.*

Hook the leaves one at a time. If leaves overlap, start with the leaf on top and then work toward the one hidden in the shadows. Decide how dark this first value must be. The leaf on top might range from a medium light to a tint, and the leaf underneath from a dark to a medium value. The same principles are applied to flower petals.

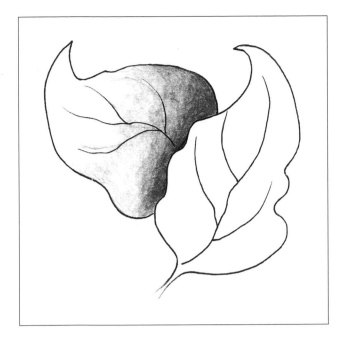

Hooking Stems

Make sure the stem is connected to the flowers and the leaves, because flowers and leaves floating apart from their stems are disconcerting. Even if they don't connect visually because a leaf or some other element is in the way, be sure the portion of the stem that is visible can be connected to the flower or the leaf by the viewer's imagination.

Hook the stems with bends, as they are rarely straight. Arrange them carefully if you are drawing your own design. A stem can lead you to your focal point, so pay attention to the way the leaves come off the stem. Do

Turnovers

A turnover is when the underside of a leaf is visible, and showing someone how to hook one can be easier than describing it. Turnovers don't need to be problematic.

Technically the underside of a leaf is light. However, we do not always interpret it that way. What I tell my students is this: Decide whether your turnover is light or dark based on the rug's background and the color of the body of the leaf. The value that is in the turnover must be carried through the turn. Let me say that again: The value that is in the turnover must be carried through the turn. This is the secret to making the leaf flip.

Think of the spot where the turnover occurs as an X, and carry the value through that spot. If you think of the X as a crossroad or a bridge, all it takes is one row of the same value going across the bridge. If you master this technique, all of your leaves will turn over realistically.

Overlaps

Where one leaf overlaps another there will always be a shadow.

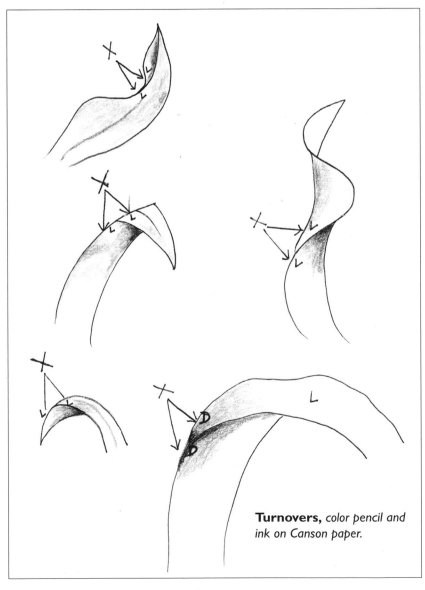

Turnovers, *color pencil and ink on Canson paper.*

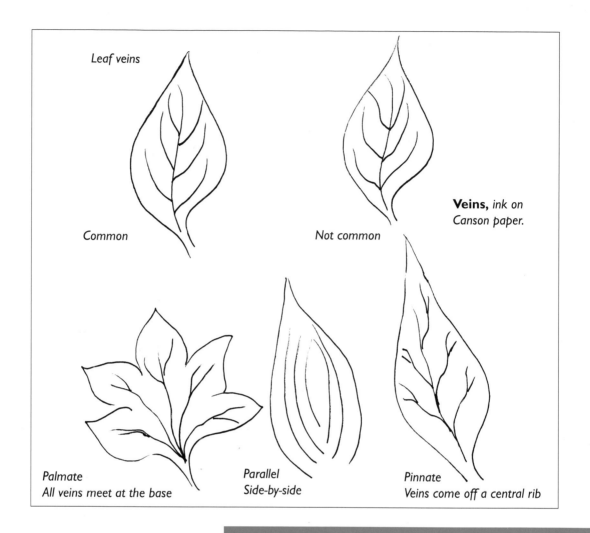

Leaf veins

Common

Not common

Veins, *ink on Canson paper.*

Palmate
All veins meet at the base

Parallel
Side-by-side

Pinnate
Veins come off a central rib

they alternate or are they exactly opposite each other? Stems look best if they are hooked with a spot dye or an over-dyed tweed. Poppy stems, for instance, are hairy, and an over-dyed tweed is the perfect material.

Hooking Veins

In designing a rug always draw the veins first. Start with the central vein, called the mid-rib, then surround the veins with the leaf shape. Do not forget to connect the veins to one another. A disconnected vein will lead to confusion.

In most cases, the veins are not positioned directly across from each other off the mid-rib. Instead, they are juxtaposed down the vein. There are a few exceptions, but when in doubt hook veins in this unbalanced manner. The vein illustration shows this principle, along with the directional flow of veining.

Favorite Leaf Dye Formulas

Pick any of these tried-and-true dye formulas for spectacular leaf colors.

Safari Green Spot Dye

This soft bronze green is suitable for primitive designs and smaller leaves. Dye it over 1 yard of natural or light green wool.
¼ tsp. Bronze (C) dissolved in 1 c. hot water
¼ tsp. Bronze Green (C) dissolved in 1 c. hot water
¼ tsp. Bright Green (C) dissolved in 1 c. hot water
¼ tsp. Chartreuse (C) dissolved in 2 c. hot water, poured over the entire piece

Primary Fusion #33

Use this soft olive green in almost any floral rug.
⅛ tsp. Yellow #119 (PC)
1/16 tsp. Black #672 (PC)
Dissolve both dyes in 1 cup of hot water and create a gradation.

Maine Leaf

Try this casserole-dyed wool for any colorful leaf.
¼ tsp. Old Gold (C) dissolved in 1 c. hot water
1/16 tsp. Orange # 233 (PC) dissolved in 1 c. hot water
¼ tsp. Red #366 (PC) dissolved in 1 c. hot water

CHAPTER SEVEN

Flower Shapes—Bells and Hearts

"The temple bell stops, but I still hear the sound coming out of the flower."—Basho

The flowers in this chapter follow the three-dimensional shape of a bell. The stem supports the flower from the top and the blossoms fall around the axis of the stamen. When seen from the side, the petal edges appear light against the dark interior of the bell. The stems are prone to bending over.

Bleeding Heart (*Lamprocapnor*)

These fairy tale flowers dangling from a single vine have the unique shape of a heart hanging down like a bell. The red-and-white flowers are bright, and in large clusters they create magnificent accents of color in a landscape. They are also called lady's locket and lady in the boat, titles whose origins become apparent when the wings are pulled apart and the flower held upside down. Bleeding hearts are not the most common flower in rug hooking, but they do deserve more attention.

Colors: Red, pink, or white

Petals: The small blossoms, 1" to 2" in size, look like little drops of blood. Each stem has six or more individual blossoms. The flower consists of an upper petal, which is light with a crease running through the center, two darker side petals that flip upward, and three bottom petals. In a red or pink bleeding heart, the bottom outer petals are colored and the center one is white. In a white bleeding heart, the lower center section is yellow. Between the upper and lower petals is a white or yellow triangle-shaped area that is a continuation of the lower center.

Leaves and stems: The leaves are fernlike and lobed. The arching stems are deeply embedded between the two sides of the heart.

Rating: 1

Challenge: None

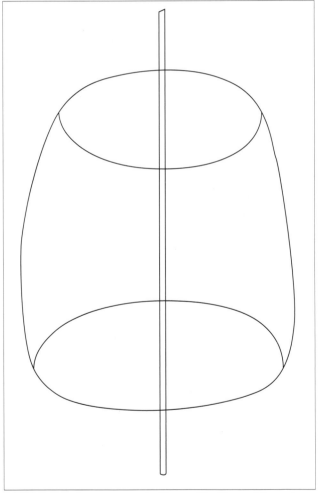

Geometric representation of bell- and heart-shaped flowers, *ink on Canson paper.*

Materials: A bleeding heart can be hooked with a minimum of two values of color and a bit of white. The scrap bin will yield exactly what you need.

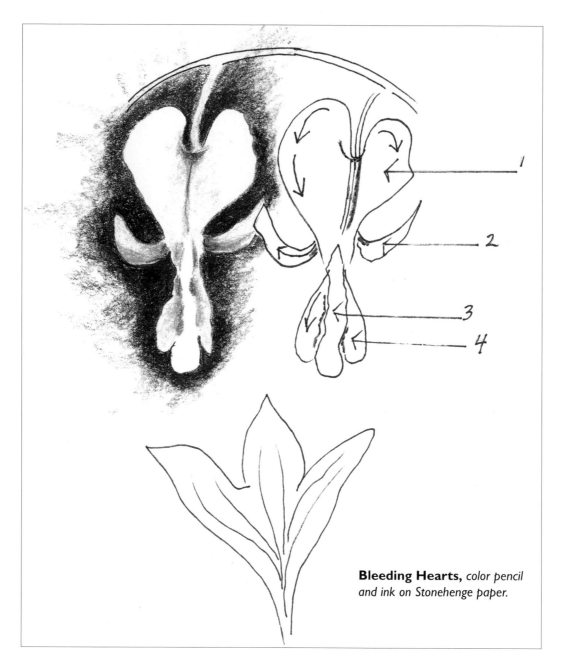

Bleeding Hearts, *color pencil and ink on Stonehenge paper.*

How to Hook

This is a very small flower, so keep the loops inside the lines.

1. Start with the largest front petal. Hook the crease down the center with a medium light to medium value.
2. Fill in the front petal with the lightest value.
3. Hook the side petals. These petals flip upward. Use darker values, especially at the point where they join the front petal.
4. Hook the center white. This area is below the largest front petal.
5. The outer petals on either side of the white center require a dark value.
6. Attach the stem to the top.

Canterbury Bells (*Campanula*)

Canterbury bells, also known as campanula, bell flower, or coventry bells have a flat base and are often referred to as cup and saucer flowers. Beekeepers use these plants to attract bees.

Colors: Blue, lavender, pink, white, and purple

Petals: The blossom is a single bell with five scallops around the edge and a flat bottom. There are noticeable veins along the elongated tube.

Flower center: The center is yellow-green, yellow, or orange depending on the particular specimen.

Leaves and stems: The leaves are long and wavy with saw-like edges. The plant grows 3' to 4' tall on a stalk in a spike-like fashion.

Rating: 2

Canterbury Bells, *color pencil and ink on Stonehenge paper.*

Challenge: Shadows within the interior and under the lip have to be dark enough to define the flower. If you get this part right, then the rest is relatively easy.

Materials: Three values of light, medium, and dark.

How to Hook

Primitive approach: Hook the lip light, the interior dark, and the long tube medium.

1. Start with the stamen and pistils. Surround them with the darkest value of your chosen color.

2. Hook the lightest lip.
3. Hook along the underside of the turned-back lip with the darkest value.
4. Hook the sepals at the base of the tube.
5. Hook the veins on the longest tube lengthwise. Try a medium value first. Fill around the veins with a lighter value down the center, and go darker where the flower turns into shadow at the sides.

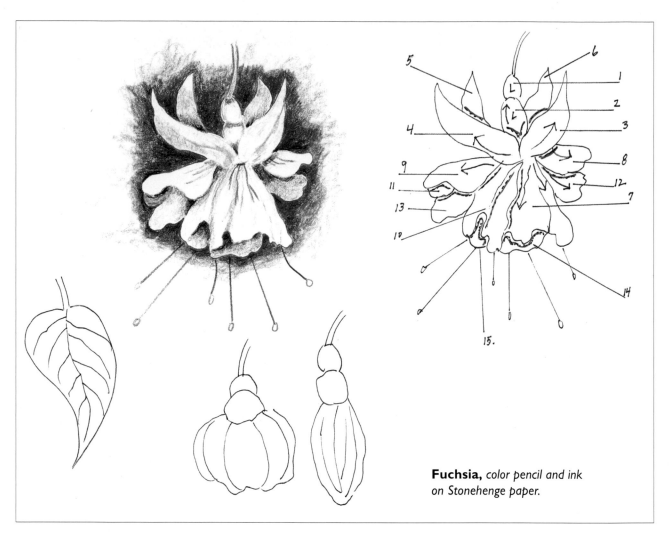

Fuchsia, *color pencil and ink on Stonehenge paper.*

Fuchsia (*Fuchsia*)

Fuchsias grow as small shrubs and come in an endless variety of colors. The shrubs blanket the countryside, painting the hillsides with a strong red and purple haze. Thousands of these tiny flowers blooming together are a marvelous sight. When the blossoms are open, they look like bells.

Colors: The entire flower may be red, purple, white, or pink. In many instances, the upper petals are one color and lower ones another. A good visual aid is important while color planning a fuchsia.

Petals: The petals overlap and look like bells wearing upturned hats. The stamens are long and pink, and the throat or neck at the top of the flower is long. Tiny blossoms hang below the stem, their petals turning in a dainty frill around an inner bell. Stamen tips are red.

Buds: Two buds are shown in the illustration. Some buds are fat and look like small pumpkins on a stem; others are longer and rounded at the tip.

Flower centers: Long stamens come out from below. If you draw a fuchsia, the stamens should always be different lengths.

Leaves and stems: There is a prominent yellow-green receptacle connecting the blossom to the stem. The leaf veins are red, and the stems are a reddish brown. The leaves are narrow, oval, and smooth. The charming red veins and stems are a distinguishing characteristic of the plant. Play this up in your work.

Rating: 6

Challenge: Hooking the fuchsia is harder than it looks. The overlapping petals, ruffles, and twists of the lower part of the flower are the primary challenge.

Materials: Two swatches are necessary unless the drawing is miniature.

How to Hook

The actual blossom is petite. Enlarging it makes hooking easier and results in a more dramatic piece.

1. Start with the receptacle. The highlight is in the center and should be light.
2. Hook the upper petals.
3. Hook the lower petals. I call this the skirt. Tackle the lightest ones first and save the dark petals underneath, called the petticoat, for last.

Self Discovery, *24" x 20", #3- and 4-cut wool on linen. Designed by Jane Halliwell Green and hooked by Elissa Crouch, Cambridge, Maryland, 2011.*

Elissa Crouch hooked a magnificent and greatly enlarged flower. It is hard to believe the actual size of a fuchsia is the size of a thumb when gazing at this one! The flower was cross-swatched with two pink-and-purple 6-value swatches.

The background is a noodle background, described in Chapter 4. All the spirals were hooked with light values of green, blue-green, and blue. These were surrounded by medium values and then darks of the same colors. The cool background supports the magnificent and warm flower. Notice that one band is hooked in the same strong pink as the flower and leads the eye to the focal point.

Lily of the Valley (*Convallaria magalis*)

The old-fashioned lily of the valley, with its broad leaves and fragrant, nodding, white, bell-shaped flowers, is very familiar. It is one of the first spring flowers emerging in a coil-like fashion from underneath the dead winter leaves. It is known by other names including May lily, Our Lady's tears, lily constancy, ladder-to-heaven, and Jacob's ladder. Although a lily of the valley looks delicate, it is tough as nails and thrives in shade and small places.

Colors: Colors are limited to white and pale pink.

Petals: The blossoms are fragrant and grow in clusters. The edges of the flower turn upward; the stalks have multiple blossoms.

Lily of the Valley, *color pencil and ink on Stonehenge paper.*

Mother's Garden, *detail. See full rug on page 124.*

Leaves and stems: The leaves are wide, smooth, glossy, and linear with veins running lengthwise from the base to the tip. They often fold inward. The stems are light olive green. An interesting note for dyers out there: the leaves will provide a natural green dye if soaked in lime water.

Rating: 2

Challenge: This is a fairly easy flower with three main challenges: 1) The background should be dark enough to create a contrast between background and flower, 2) multiple blossoms should be hooked progressively darker as they move down the stem (each blossom casts a shadow on the one beneath it, and 3) most designs will require a #3 or #4 cut, which may be a challenge for those who are not used to hooking with such a narrow strip.

Materials: A soft white spot dye or a 3- to 4-value white swatch is a perfect choice.

How to Hook

Primitive approach: Outline and fill each blossom with a white spot dye. Hook a strip of gray between the overlapping flowers.

Finely shaded: Start with the flower at the top of the stem and hook the entire flower with your lightest value. Progressively get darker as you move down the stem. Where overlaps occur, slip in a very dark shadow. Instead of hooking a complete line, try a loop/a tail/a loop in two places so the shadow line is broken up and will not appear too linear. Keep in mind that the petal edges will be lightest where they flip upward.

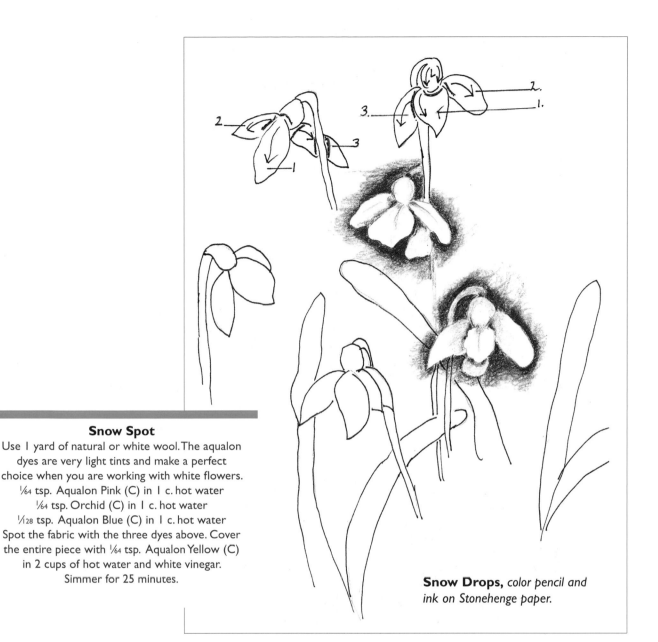

Snow Drops, *color pencil and
ink on Stonehenge paper.*

Snow Drops (*Galanthus*)

> *"Many, many welcomes,*
> *February fair maid."*
> —Alfred Lord Tennyson

As the name suggests, this flower may not even wait for
the snow to melt before pushing up through the ground.
The 75 species of this flower look like three drops of
milk hanging from a stem. Some people refer to it as the
"milk flower."

Color: White

Petals: The six petals droop down off the stem. The
outer petals have a yellow-green marking on the lower
edge. Unless the flower is designed as an oversized close
up, these markings can be ignored.

Flower center: You must look into the flower to see

this area, which is green and gold.

Leaves and stems: This flower has long, thin stems
with strap leaves. The end of the leaf is curved rather
than pointed.

Rating: 1

Challenge: None. This is a good first flower.

Materials: White spot dye or a 3- to 4-value swatch

How to Hook

1. Start with the receptacle and stem. Hook them in
   yellow green.
2. Hook the top petal first with lightest values.
3. Follow this with the petals on each side.
4. In some flowers, you'll see a fourth or fifth petal come
   from behind. These are the darkest petals. ☙

CHAPTER EIGHT

Flower Shapes—Cups, Bowls, and Spheres

"I will be the gladdest thing / Under the sun! / I will touch a hundred flowers, / And not pick one."—Edna St. Vincent Millay, "Afternoon on a Hill"

The flowers in this section have a round appearance. Buttercups have the simplest shape, presenting a gentle curve of petals that form a circle when viewed face on. The buds are rounded and the fully opened flowers are shaped like bowls. (Roses and tulips, which are covered later, are shaped like teacups.)

Buttercup (*Ranunculus*)

When spring arrives these bright yellow blossoms, about the size of a quarter, show up on lawns and roadsides.

Color: Bright yellow

Petals: At the base of five small, lustrous petals lies a cuplike scale. It contains a secret pool of nectar that insects seek out. This is called the nectariferous spot, or pit, and is the key to whether the little yellow flower is a true buttercup.

Flower center: The center is the most interesting part of the flower. Buttercups have a yellow-green center composed of a cluster of pistils and stamens. Yellow anthers surround the center.

Leaves and stems: The leaves are triangular and lobed with ragged edges.

Rating: 1. This is a good flower for a beginner.

Challenge: The distinguishing characteristic of the flower is the fancy center so that needs be the dominant feature.

Materials: 2- to 4-value swatch

How to Hook

1. Start with the petals, and save the center for last.
2. There is very little overlap between each of the five petals. A simple approach is to fill each petal with a single value.

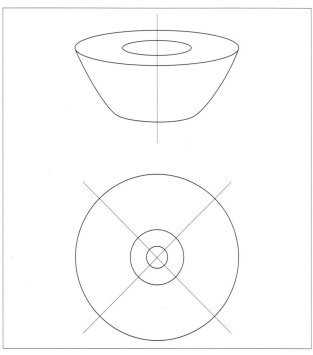

Geometric representation of cup, bowl, and spherical flowers, *ink on Canson paper.*

A 5-value swatch was used for the wall hanging, *Buttercup Twins*. Each petal was hooked in two values with a dark yellow-green separating one petal from another. A yellow-green organza ribbon was hooked last in the dramatic center.

You might pixelate the middle with a yellow-green tweed or plaid and surround it with DMC embroidery floss or yarn. If you choose embroidery thread, sew, rather than hook the threads, by knotting them in the back of your work and clipping the threads at the surface.

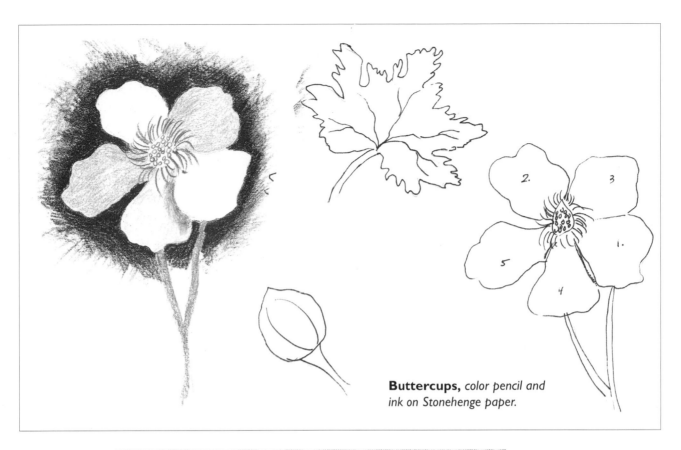

Buttercups, *color pencil and ink on Stonehenge paper.*

Buttercup Twins,
*14" x 17", #4- and 5-
cut wool and ribbon on
linen. Designed and
hooked by Jane Halliwell
Green, Edgewater,
Maryland, 2011.*

Dancing Cyclamen, 18" x 22", #3-cut wool on cotton warp cloth. Designed and hooked by Jane Halliwell Green, Edgewater, Maryland, 2011.

Rating: 6

Challenge: You'll face two with this flower: capturing the markings on the leaves and shading the overlapping and upright blossoms.

Materials: An 8-value swatch with an additional piece of dark purple for the markings at the base of the petal was used in *Dancing Cyclamen*.

Cyclamen (*Cyclamen Persicum*)

Cyclamens are Christmas plants that flower for many months. The blossoms resemble pink butterflies hovering above the stems and leaves as they reach for the sky. I love the large rounded leaves with their wonderful markings. Unfortunately, cyclamens do not find their way into many rugs. Hopefully including them here will result in many more fiber cyclamens.

Colors: Hot pink, rose and white, red, and purple

Petals: The five petals are tulip-shaped but they do not overlap tightly. The dark patch at the base of the petal is red-violet or purple. The buds drop downward or outward, rarely upward.

Leaves and stamens: The leaves are distinctively heart-shaped with sawlike edges and strong patterning—a distinguishing characteristic of the cyclamen. The spreading veins and lighter patches of color toward the outside edge of the leaf garner more attention than the showy blossoms. The stems are tall, slender, and slightly pink. Each blossom and leaf has its own stem leading from the base of the plant.

How to Hook

Dancing Cyclamen was hooked with a #3 cut. This flower lends itself to more realistic shading.

1. Start with the front petal. Hook from the dark purple base to the light tip. The dark purple patch appears only at the base of the front petals. Use Primary Fusion #10 and Fireworks spot dye.
2. Select medium and dark values, and proceed to hook the petals in the rear.
3. Hook the stems in a dull beige-pink.
4. The leaves are as challenging as the flowers. Because the sawlike edges are difficult to hook, they were made to look smooth. Hook the leaf markings and veins first.
5. Use the dip dyes in the dancing roots. Dye them over natural wool measuring 12" x 18".
6. The background was Dorr Mill's Eggplant. I used a combination of wool directly off the bolt and the same wool over dyed with ¼ teaspoon #672 Black (PC). Hook it in swirling lines.

Primary Fusion #10—Pink petals

⅛ tsp. Magenta # 338 (PC)
1/128 tsp. Black #672 (PC)
Dissolve both dyes in 1 c. of water
and create an 8-value gradation.

Fireworks, Spot Dye—Base of front petals

1 yd. of natural or pink wool
¼ tsp. Red-Violet (MC)
dissolved in 1 c. hot water
1/4 tsp. Blue Violet (MC)
dissolved in 1 c. hot water
¼ tsp. Blue (MC) dissolved in 1 c. hot water

Summer Green, Spot Dye

⅛ tsp. Blue (MC) dissolved in 1 c. hot water
⅛ tsp. Moss Green (MC)
dissolved in 1 c. hot water
⅛ tsp. Bottle Green (MC)
dissolved in 1 c. hot water
⅛ tsp. Brilliant Green (MC)
dissolved in 1 c. hot water
⅛ tsp. Yellow (MC) dissolved in 2 c. water
and white vinegar. Pour this final color
over the entire yard of fabric.

Botanical Surprise, Fry Pot

¼ tsp. Yellow #135 (PC)
dissolved in 1 c. hot water
1/32 tsp. Green # 728 (PC)
dissolved in 1 c. hot water
1/32 tsp. Forest Green #725 (PC)
dissolved in 1 c. hot water
1/32 tsp. Turquoise #478 (PC)
dissolved in 1 c. water

Cyclamen Lilac, Fry Pot

1/64 tsp. Black #672 (PC)
dissolved in 1 c. hot water
1/128 tsp. Blue #490 (PC) dissolved in 1 c. hot water
1/64 tsp. Forest Green #725 (PC)
dissolved in 1 c. hot water
1/32 tsp. Lilac #845 (PC) dissolved in 1 c. hot water

WFS #50 Aurora, Spot Dye

1/64 tsp. Blue #490 (PC) and
1/128 tsp. Black #672 (PC)
dissolved in 1 c. hot water
1/128 tsp. Navy #413 (PC) and 1/128 tsp. Black #672
(PC) dissolved in 1 c. hot water

Cyclamen, *color pencil and ink on Stonehenge paper.*

Fancy Roots #1

1/64 tsp. Yellow #199 (PC)
dissolved in 1 c. hot water and placed in Pan 1
1/64 tsp. Fuchsia #349 (PC)
dissolved in 1 c. hot water and placed in Pan 2
1/64 tsp. Blue Violet (MC)
dissolved in 1 c. hot water and placed in Pan 3

Fancy Roots #2

1/64 tsp. Yellow #199 (PC)
dissolved in 1 c. hot water and placed in Pan 1
1/64 tsp. Green #725 (PC)
dissolved in 1 c. hot water and placed in Pan 2
1/128 tsp. Turquoise #478 (PC)
dissolved in 1 c. hot water and placed in Pan 3

Gardenia (*Gardenia*)

"Gardenias can link our souls with the divine."
—William Howard Adams

The gardenia originated in China and is a member of the coffee family. Both my mother and I carried a bouquet of gardenias when we were married. Needless to say, they are my family's favorite flower. These tropical plants are difficult to grow in colder climates. Distinguishing features are their strong scent and their waxy yellow-white petals.

Colors: White and pale yellow

Petals: Five to twelve petals are arranged in a spiral.

Flower center: The small petals are curled up tightly in the center, and the darkest shadows surround them.

Leaves and stems: The leaves are smooth, shiny, and oval. The dark green leaves are glossy.

Rating: 6

Challenge: A white flower is always a challenge because you must tint the petals with enough color to create shadows yet still end up with what appears to be a white flower. Remember that white objects are in fact at least 75% color and 25% white.

Materials: Use a 6- to 8-value swatch

How to Hook

Use mock shading for a gardenia. Because the petals are not as deep as those of a rose, it is easier to hook in curved horizontal lines rather than in vertical lines. Place the dark values at the base of the petals, gradually getting lighter at the petal's edge. When two petals are side by side or back to front, the light part of one pushes against the dark edge of the other.

1. Start by placing the darkest values around the tiny, bunched-up center petals. Since this is your darkest area, everything else will be lighter.
2. Proceed to the outer circle of petals and work back toward the center. Hook light to dark values in curved horizontal lines. Avoid "stripyness" by juxtaposing closely related values within the petal.
3. Take a photograph. This will indicate whether the flower has enough depth. If the petals seem to blur together, place dark values between them.

White Magic
This formula was inspired by the result one gets by floating watercolors on wet paper.
Use ½ yard of white wool for each value.

⅟₃₂ tsp. Yellow #119 (PC)
dissolved in 1 c. hot water
⅟₃₂ tsp. Magenta #338 (PC)
dissolved in 1 c. hot water
⅟₃₂ tsp. Blue #490 (PC)
dissolved in 1 c. hot water

Value 1

🐋 Place the wool in the dye pot, and bring the heat up to a simmer. Add 1 tablespoon of the yellow, and let it float down upon the wool.

🐋 Turn the fabric. Do the same with 1 tablespoon of pink and 1 tablespoon of blue, carefully turning your fabric. Add white vinegar.

Value 2

🐋 Float 2 tablespoons of the pink and yellow.

🐋 Float 3 tablespoons of the blue.

Value 3

🐋 Float 4 tablespoons of each color.

Value 4

🐋 Float 8 tablespoons of each color.

Gardenia, *color pencil and ink on Stonehenge paper.*

Fig, Prisms #115
1/32 tsp. Brown #503 (PC)
1/128 tsp. Yellow #135 (PC)
Dissolve both dyes in 1 c. of hot water
and create a gradation.

Jane's Gray
1/4 tsp. Black #672 (PC)
dissolved in 1 c. hot water

Magnolia, *color pencil and ink on Stonehenge paper.*

Magnolia (*Magnolia*)

Magnolias are dramatic and grow on large trees. Preprinted patterns are readily available, and the flower is simple to draw and to hook.

Colors: White, pink, and combinations of both

Petals: The large, tulip-shaped petals range from 3" to 12" in diameter and may be light pink or purple within the interior. The outside edges are smooth and have a tendency to flip upward. A magnolia that folds upward resembles a cyclamen.

Flower center: Try shagging or sculpting the center,

which will give the flower dimension and catch the viewer's eye. The color of the center can be yellow-green, pink, orange, or gold.

Leaves and stems: The leaves look stiff. They are oval, smooth, shiny, and attached to a heavy tree branch.

Rating: 3

Challenge: The challenge here is to add just enough dark value between the petals without losing the appearance of a white flower.

Materials: Dip dyes plus an additional dark value for the shadows

Mammoth Flower Pillow, Magnolia #9, *16" square, ripped strips of wool on linen. Designed by Jeanette Fraser and hooked by Jane Halliwell Green, Edgewater, Maryland, 2011.*

How to Hook

Almost any dark background will look good behind a magnolia.

1. Start with the center. In *Mammoth Flower Pillow*, the spot dye called Everything Spot was used in the center. Loops were pulled up high and left that way. This technique is called *loop shagging*. If you prefer, the loops can be *sculpted* (trimmed and shaped) for a fuzzier appearance.

2. Next, turn your attention to the lightest petal. If you are working with a dip dye, play with the strip to get an acceptable flow of color. The dipped strip may be a perfect fit for the longest part of the petal, but the inner and shorter part of the petal may require piecing and clipping to get the color flow you want.

3. Continue to hook each petal moving backward toward the darkest ones. Use the additional dark value for the shadowed areas between petals and under the turnovers.

Everything Spot
Dye this delightful color over
1 yard of natural, yellow, or peach wool.
1 tsp. #199 Yellow (PC)
dissolved in 1 c. hot water
¼ tsp. Maroon (C) dissolved in 1 c. hot water
¼ tsp. Navy (PC) dissolved in 1 c. water
Place the navy spots carefully on the wool so that
they do not completely cover the gold spots.

Dyeing for a Pink and White Magnolia
Use white wool for this dye formula. This will give you a gorgeous magnolia. Primary Fusion #11 is the dark end of the dip, Pink #2 is the center of the dip, and the white end of the fabric was dipped in ¹⁄₁₆ teaspoon Champagne (C) to tone down the harshness of the white.

Primary Fusion #11
¼ tsp. Magenta #338 (PC)
¹⁄₆₄ tsp. Black #672 (PC)
¹⁄₁₂₈ tsp. Blue #490 (PC)
Dissolve all dyes in 1 c. of hot water.

Pink #2
¼ tsp. Old Rose (C)
¹⁄₃₂ tsp. Silver Gray (C)
¹⁄₃₂ tsp. Aqualon Blue (C)
All dyes are dissolved in 1 c. of hot water.

Peony, *color pencil and ink on Stonehenge paper.*

Peony (*Paeonia*)

"I have a garden of my own,
Shining with flowers of every hue;
I love it dearly while alone,
But I shall love it more with you."
—Thomas Moore

In 1903, the peony was declared the national flower of China, where it is called the king of flowers, or the flower fairy. The flowers are a symbol of wealth, luck, and happiness. The plant is a shrub that produces large and magnificent flowers. There are numerous species with different shapes—some spherical, others cup-shaped.

Because of their numerous overlapping petals, they are difficult to hook. The cup-shaped peony is the easiest to render in fiber.

Colors: Red, pink, white, yellow, and pale orange

Petals: There are many overlapping petals which look like golf balls. Many sepals hang down from both the petals and the buds.

Flower center: Gold, white, and yellow-green with numerous stamens.

Leaves and stems: Depending on the variety, peonies exhibit almost every leaf shape—triangular, oval, or squiggly.

Karen, *24" x 36",*
#3-cut wool on
monk's cloth.
Designed by
Jane McGown Flynn
and hooked by
Cyndra Mogayzel,
Annapolis, Maryland,
2011.

Rating: 8

Challenge: Overlapping petals and turnovers provide a real challenge.

Materials: One or two 8-value swatches

How to Hook

A single rather than double variety is easier to hook. The drawing represents a single cup-shaped peony.

1. Start in the center with the darkest values. Everything else will be lighter.
2. Next, hook the lightest turnovers in a tint. The space is usually narrow and requires horizontal hooking.
3. Move to the lightest front petals, and hook these in light to medium values. Try to maintain a curved vertical line to mimic the way the plant grows and to achieve the cupped effect so distinctive of a peony.
4. Continue back toward the center with medium to dark values.

Cyndra Mogazyel created a gorgeous peony in the rug *Karen.*

Poppies, *color pencil and ink on Stonehenge paper.*

Poppy (*Papaver*)

"Once you have seen a field of rice-paper-thin poppies blowing gently in the breeze, your perception of them changes."
—Elissa Crouch, Eastern Shore of Maryland rug hooker

The Oriental poppy, native to Northeastern Iran and Turkey, is a favorite in rug hooking. The Himalayan blue poppy is rarely hooked, but is an unusual and stunning flower. The Icelandic or California poppy is recognized for its heavily crinkled petals and ruffles in addition to its characteristic golden yellow hue.

Colors: The original Oriental poppy was red. Other colors have appeared, including white, salmon pink, and dark maroon. Himalayan Poppies are an intense medium blue and are almost azure-like. The Icelandic or California poppy has golden-yellow petals with a yellow-orange base.

Petals: Poppy flowers resemble smocked dresses with many creases. Blossoms can be as wide as 8". The buds are oval with hairs covering their entire surface.

Flower center: A large rounded center dome surrounded by spikes sits in the center of the poppy and is red-violet or mauve. Hook the center with an over-dyed black and white check. The spikes around the dome are either a dark purple or black. Select a true black or eggplant for this area. Black threads or yarn can be an interesting choice for a wall hanging. The center of a Himalayan blue poppy is gold or orange with a bit of yellow-green. The center of the California poppy is yellow.

Poppies and Daisies Close-Up, *40"x 42", #8-cut and hand-ripped wool strips on linen. Designed by Jane Halliwell Green and hooked by Cyndra Mogayzel, Annapolis, Maryland, 2011.*

Leaves and stems: The stems are hairy and bend under the weight of the flowers. Use tweeds to get this hairy look or over dye a gray and white houndstooth check with a green dye. The leaves of an Oriental poppy are narrow and lobed, with sawlike edges that look like ferns. The Icelandic Poppy has lobed leaves, but they are smooth.

Rating: 7

Challenge: First, the petals can turn upward or downward. Therefore each artist must make a decision regarding the placement of values. Each flower can hold a different pose. Second, the poppy is loaded with crinkles and ruffles. Indentifying the right value for these shadows is a challenge. In most cases, a medium value works, but it is a process of trial and error and an occasional need to "reverse hook."

Materials: Choose dip dyes plus an extra shadow color for a large poppy and a 6- to 8-value swatch for a smaller poppy.

How to Hook

The poppy is a tricky flower to hook, so provide yourself with a road map by writing directional arrows and values on the backing.

1. Start with the center dome. Hook this with a black check.
2. If thread or yarn is planned for the spikes around the dome, leave a space and come back later.
3. Finish each petal before going on to the next one.
4. Hook the creases first. Make your best guess on the value. Medium values usually provide enough

Pitcher Poppies,
*20" x 16", #3-cut
wool on linen.
Designed by
Jane Halliwell Green
and hooked by Elissa
Crouch, Cambridge,
Maryland, 2010.*

103B Prisms
This two-color formula
is a favorite
for an Oriental poppy.

First color
1/32 tsp. Orange #233 (PC)
dissolved in 1 c. hot water

Second color
1/4 tsp. Red #351 (PC)
1/8 tsp. Orange #233 (PC)
1/32 tsp. Chestnut #560 (PC)
1/128 tsp. Blue #425C (PC)
Dissolve all four dyes in 1 c. of
hot water.

contrast against a light petal. The same is true for dark values against medium petals.

5. Start with the first petal. In the drawing, the front petal flips upward toward the center. You can start with the darker edge and work up toward the top edge, or start at the top and work down. Because of its shape, establish the curve by hooking a curved, vertical line in the middle of the petal and then work outward toward the edges.

6. Continue with each petal in order. The smaller petals on top of the larger ones can be hooked with one or two values.

Cyndra Mogayzel tackled a large close-up rug with 1" ripped strips (*see page 53*). This magnificent rug is bold and bright.

Elissa Crouch hooked *Pitcher Poppies*, a finely shaded wall hanging. Elissa cross-swatched the fabrics in this painterly approach. The fabric used for the pitcher was cut and hooked as it came off the cutter, one section at a time. In this way, the washed and abrashed effect on the fabric's surface would be evident. The background was a dark neutral with shots of color that make it sparkle yet do not compete with the design.

Rose (Rosa)

The rose holds a special position in the rug hooking world and appears in many of our floral designs. Historically, rose fossils have been found in Colorado dating back 35 million years. Ancient Sumerians of Mesopotamia mentioned roses in a cuneiform tablet written in approximately 2860 BC.

So many varieties of this popular flower are available. In this section we will focus on a classification called Old Garden Roses. The description that follows relates to the classic cup and saucer, and cabbage roses.

Colors: Unlimited

Petals: The large curved outside petals get smaller toward the center.

Flower centers: The darkest value is in the center of a tea rose.

Leaves and stems: Ragged oval leaves grow out of thick stems covered with reddish thorns. The leaves are dark, shiny, yellow- or bronze-green. Use spot dyes or tweed for the stems. Notice the sepals growing beneath the buds and the flowers.

Rating: 5, depending on the complexity of the particular rose

Challenge: The greatest challenge awaits a new rug hooker who tackles a finely shaded rose for the first time. Try a primitive rose or the simpler mock shading first. Work with a teacher the first time you attempt this flower.

How to Hook

Rug hookers can feel intimidated when facing their first rose. Hooking a rose is like riding a bike—once you learn to do it, you'll never forget. Here are three basic ways to handle a rose. Start with the primitive technique and work toward the realistic version.

Primitive: This easy rose is very effective. Follow diagram A. Choose a color in four values for the petals. Choose an outline material. Spot dyes and plaids are good outlines. Use these two guidelines for selecting the appropriate outline:

- An outline as dark as your darkest petal value

Placement of Values in a Primitive Rose, *ink on Stonehenge paper.*

- Include the color of your chosen swatch (A plaid might be appropriate after over dyeing it in this chosen color.)

1. Outline and fill in one petal at a time. This instruction is important. If you outline every petal before hooking the interior of the petal, you will get confused. Follow the drawing and the hooking directions.
2. Even though this technique is simple, it is still important to logically place values in areas that correspond to the actual light, medium, and dark areas of the flower. In diagram (A), the letters L, M, MD, and D will guide you.
3. The order of hooking is not critical in a primitive rose because each petal is separated by an outline. In addition, shadows are not necessary.

Toni Breeding hooked this primitive rose in *Rose and Lattice*. The rug is a good example of how the method described can produce a lovely mat.

C.

Roses, *color pencil and ink on Stonehenge paper.*

B.

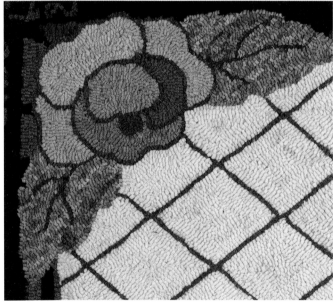

Rose and Lattice, *detail. See full rug on page 125.*

Work on the lightest outer petals and then continue into the darker recesses of the rose. Follow diagram B.

Realistic fine shading: This is the ultimate in flower shading. It is the final and most realistic shading you can do for a hooked rose. Follow diagram C.

1. Use a #3 cut.
2. It is acceptable to skip values between but not inside petals.
3. Finger multiple values together to create a flower that is "painted with wool." You'll need at least eight values, and experienced rug hookers often exceed ten.
4. Start with the lightest petal. The lightest petals are the rolls. They are narrow, so the number of values will be limited to a tint and a light. Hook the rolls along their length.
5. Next, hook the light petals along the outer perimeter of the flower. Start at the outer edges to establish the curve. Dark values lie at the base of the petal while lighter ones are at the outer edge. Hook from the outer edges inward. **Tip:** In a realistic rose it is important not to skip values within the petals. However, it is often necessary to skip values when selecting a darker material for the area between the petals.

Simple mock: Mock shading is the next step toward the realistic rose. Select four to six values. Hook in a horizontal direction with a gentle curve and place the lights, mediums, and darks side by side without the work of fingering covered in Chapter 3. Avoid a stripy look by mixing closely related values in the transition from one to the other.

Blue Moon Rose, *18" x 12", #4-cut wool on cotton rug warp. Designed and hooked by Ingrid Hieronimus, Petersburg, Ontario, Canada, 2000.* INGRID HIERONIMUS

6. Continue to hook the petals toward the center of the flower. Add dark shadows between petals as needed. The center is always the darkest part of the rose. Always maintain a curve. **Tip:** New rug hookers may find it easier to see the shading of a realistic rose by hooking the dark values first followed by the light, leaving the center empty. The medium values will be squeezed into the empty center.

Ingrid Hieronimus designed and hooked *Blue Moon Rose* to teach beginners fine shading.

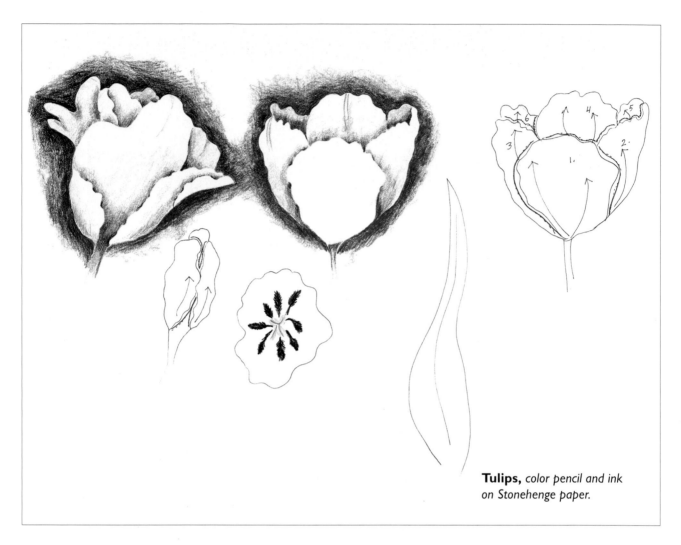

Tulips, *color pencil and ink on Stonehenge paper.*

Tulip (*Tulipa*)

"Tall tulips lift in scarlet tire, / Brimming the April dusk with fire."—Lizette Woodworth Reese

In the seventeenth century, Holland was gripped with "tulipomania." Tulips symbolize imagination and dreaminess. Fiber artists have experienced this dream by hooking hundreds of tulip rugs over the years. The smooth-edged, early blooming tulips and the ruffled parrot tulip are popular in our rugs.

Colors: Any color or color combination is possible. Tulips have been commercially bred for so many years that every hue has been created.

Petals: There are six or more petals depending on the particular variety. Some petal edges are smooth, while others such as the parrot tulip will be fringed or ruffled.

Flower centers: The interior of an open tulip is distinctive. If the tulip is open, the pistil and the stamen might be visible. The pistil is a yellow- to bronze-green, and the anthers are black or rust.

Leaves and stems: The leaves are linear and smooth and twist and turn in more than one place. Refer to

Chapter 6 for more information on turnovers.

Rating: 2

Challenge: You'll face three challenges in hooking tulips: achieving shadows that are dark enough, maintaining curved lines, and linking the front petal to the stem with a connecting fabric.

Materials: Dip dyes are the best choice for a large tulip, while swatches work better in smaller ones. Working with a combination of dips and values is always a good choice.

How to Hook

The pose of a tulip is important and dictates the steps required to hook the flower. Some flowers are completely closed; others fall wide open.

1. Always start with the front, most fully exposed petal. Hook from a dark base to a light tip. Be sure to curve the lines. **Tip:** When dipping wool for the front petal, add a touch of green that can overlap with the petal color. When you study tulips, notice that the stem's color creeps upward into the center of the front petal.

Conversations, *24½" x 24", #4-cut wool on cotton.*
Designed and hooked by Barbara Jess, Yarmouth, Nova Scotia, Canada, 2009. BELLE HATFIELD

2. Hook the side petals next. Be sure the value separating the side from the front is dark enough. It may be necessary to skip a value here.

3. Complete the flower with the dark back petals, which are often shorter. Use the dark end of the dip dye for these small back petals.

Barbara Jess hooked a very clever floral piece called *Conversations.* Barbara says the inspiration for this design was a silly autograph book verse from the 1950s:

"Tulips in the garden
Tulips in the park
The tulips I like best
Are tulips in the dark."

Barbara has fun watching people puzzle over the name of her mat, and the look on their faces when they finally recognize the silhouettes hidden within her design. Look closely at the tulips. Can you see the image underneath?

Water Lilies, *24" x 40", #3-cut wool on linen. Designed by Jane McGown Flynn and hooked by Cindy MacIntosh, New Glasgow, Nova Scotia, 2010.* CINDY MACINTOSH.

Water Lily (*Nymphaea*)

Water lilies are the crown jewels of the pond, where their strong scent is paired with the sound of water. Their botanical name is derived from the water nymphs of Greek mythology.

The lily can be solitary or form clusters that float on the surface of the water. The flowers are connected to a stem that may be hidden under the blossoms or lily pads. Most lily flowers open for three days in succession, closing at night. The lily pads are large and circular, and support the flowers. Lotuses and pond lilies are members of the same family.

Colors: Pink, white, rose, yellow, purple, red-violet, lavender, blue, and peach

Petals: Petals are spiky and overlapped with subtle veins. The number of petals in each flower varies depending on the variety. The buds sit on top of a long stem and reach for the sun.

Flower center: In an open lily the center is dramatic. The stamens are stringy and can be as long as the petal. Yellow, gold, and combinations of yellow and pink are good choices for the center.

Leaves and stems: Pads are green, maroon, and yellow. The leaves are wax coated, circular, and supported by creeping stems that extend to the bottom of the pond. These stems are often hidden but do come up above the surface of the water. There is a pie-shaped opening in the leaf and a circular area in the center. In some varieties the leaves curve up at the edges and look like pie plates. There may be dark blotches on the surface of the leaf.

Rating: 7

Challenge: The value at the base of each petal should be dark enough that the petals do not merge together in a ball shape. Each petal should be clearly visible.

Materials: 8-value swatch

How to Hook

1. Begin with the center.
2. Hook the top and outer petals first. Pay special attention to shadows between the petals. Skipping values may be necessary. If you need to go really dark, find a scrap of dark violet.
3. Hook the next layer of petals in the rear using darker values.
4. Notice that placing light against dark in each ring of petals creates the flower. ☙

Water Lily, *color pencil and ink on Stonehenge paper.*

CHAPTER NINE

Flower Shapes—Lips and Beards

"Each flower is a soul opening out to nature."—Gérard de Nerval

Draw a line through the widest petal of one of these flowers from the top to the bottom and you'll see that each side is a mirror image of the other. The petal may have tricky overlaps or curves; therefore, shadows are important in fully defining the shape these flowers take. Lipped and bearded flowers come in an almost unlimited palette of colors.

Iris (*Iris*)

"Thou art the Iris, fair amongst the fairest,
who armed with golden rod
and winged with the celestial azure, bearest
the message of some God."
—Henry Wadsworth Longfellow

The word *iris* means "rainbow," which is why irises have always been known as flowers of the rainbow. The iris is also the flower of the Greek goddess Iris, who is the messenger between gods and mortals. These elegant flowers bloom and die quickly. Their colors are so rich that in full bloom they are breathtaking.

Irises present endless possibilities for combining color, shape, and size, so deciding which variety to hook is difficult. Irises are classified into two major groups: rhizome and bulbous. Within these two groups the choices expand even more. Within the rhizome group are bearded, beardless, and crested. The tall bearded iris and the Dutch iris (beardless) are the most popular irises rendered in wool.

Colors: Irises come in almost unlimited colors and combinations

Petals: The iris blossom is made up of two distinct parts. The upright petals are called *standards,* and the lower petals are called *falls.* Each part has three petals. The petal veins are an important characteristic and should not be omitted. The value has to be just right: too dark and they will be too prominent; too light and they will disappear.

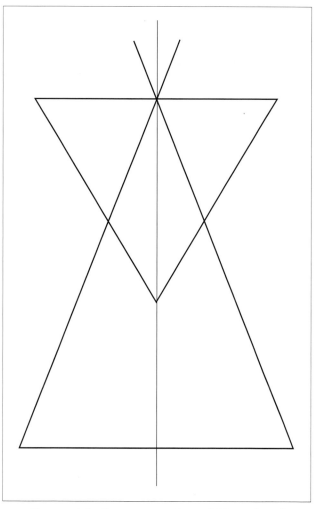

Geometric Representation of Lipped and Bearded Flowers, *ink on Canson paper.*

Flower center: The fuzzy center, which is part of the falls, is called the beard and is yellow-orange. In some varieties the beard might be white or yellow. The beard is slightly higher than the petal.

Leaves and stems: The stems have a golden top,

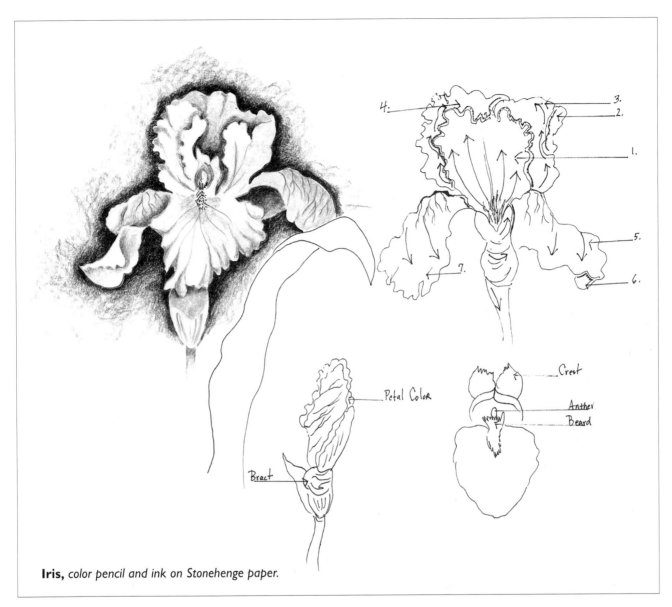

Iris, *color pencil and ink on Stonehenge paper.*

which is the bract. The leaves are tall, linear, and swordlike in shape.

Rating: 8

Challenge: An iris is a delicate flower with ruffles and turnovers galore. Therefore, it requires a smaller cut (#3 or #4) and careful attention to keeping the wool inside the lines of the drawing. It is my personal opinion that an iris is the most difficult flower to hook. Due to both the complexity and delicacy of this plant, iris designs have been oversimplified. Work from a visual aid. Make the edges interesting because they are not round and smooth. Try to capture as many of the details as possible. This flower is not the best choice for a primitive rug.

Materials: Two or more swatches are recommended.

How to Hook

1. Plan your colors. The standards can be hooked in one swatch and the falls in another. Separate two swatches into light and dark values. Hook the light values from each swatch in the standards, and the dark ones in the falls. This technique is called cross-swatching.

2. The standards are usually hooked first followed by the falls.

3. The direction of your hooking is crucial: use upward strokes for the standards and downward strokes for the falls. If you follow the direction of the veins you will be going in the right direction.

4. There is no right or wrong way to control values. Consider the pose of your flower and decide where to place light and dark values. The falls could be hooked dark near the beard to light on the bottom edges of the petals. The opposite way is fine as well.

5. Start with the beard. Sculpt or shag the beard.

6. Hook the veins and ruffles first, and place the values of your swatch between.

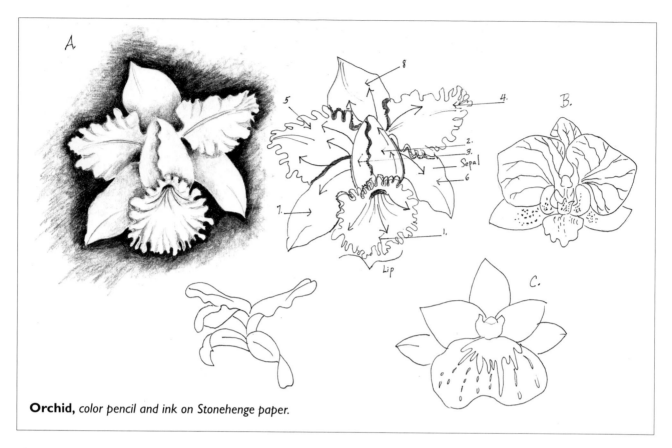

Orchid, *color pencil and ink on Stonehenge paper.*

Orchid (*Orchidaceae*)

Orchids are one of the most exquisite and fascinating flowers in the world. Many countries have adopted particular varieties as their national flower. They make up the world's most diverse plant family with the number of species estimated between 30,000 and 40,000. You can find them on all continents except Antarctica.

The basic orchid is composed of an ovary, three sepals, two petals, a lip, and a column, but the shapes and sizes vary from one species to the next. The orchid illustration shows three common types of orchids. The colors associated with each type vary, but the leaves are similar. A) The cattleya is a showy plant with frilly blossoms. Its shape is more tubular and is reminiscent of a daffodil. Common colors are orange, yellow, and red. A cattleya is the most familiar orchid in rug hooking. B) Phalaeopsis orchids are popular houseplants. They are easy to grow and are available in pink, white, red, and combinations of all three. C) Miltoniopsis orchids are pansy orchids. Their color combinations are almost unlimited.

Colors: Red, pink, yellow, white, blue, red-violet, and numerous combinations

Petals: The petal veins and spots are prominent in phalaeopsis orchids and distinguish them from other types of orchids. These petals are smooth. The petals of the cattleya are ruffled. The smooth edges found on the

sepals are often mislabeled as petals. The smooth-edged petals of the pansy orchid look like a real pansy that needs to go on a diet.

Flower center: Centers vary widely depending on the particular orchid.

Leaves and stems: The leaves are waxy, broad, linear, and twisted. They are shorter than strap leaves.

Rating: 1 or 8

🍂 Pansy orchids are the easiest to hook with a rating of 1.

🍂 Phalaeopsis and cattleya orchids are more challenging with a rating of 8.

Challenge: Hooking the shadows in the ruffles and capturing the distinguishing marks of each flower are your two challenges.

Materials: 6- to 8-value swatch

How to Hook

Get a good reference for the cattleya flower before you start. The order of hooking the petals and sepals, plus the placement of values, is dependent on the variety you choose.

1. Start in the center of the flower within the area called the lip. Notice the upside-down curve (frown) in the center with the very dark shadow inside. Hook this first. Next, create the ruffles around the edges of the lip. Finally, finish adding the main color by hooking

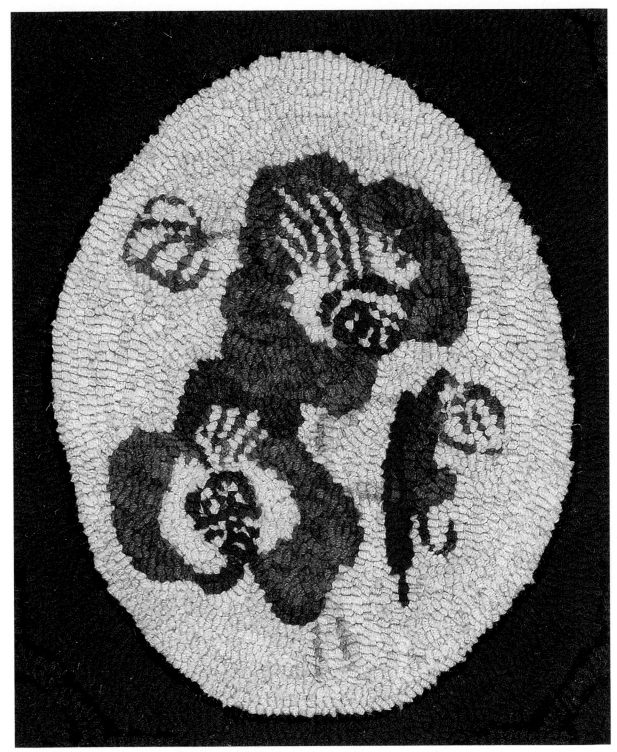

Mother's Garden, *detail. See full rug on page 124.*

from the frown outward toward the edge.

2. Next, hook the tube behind the lip. Place the center shadow and the one underneath the lip first. Fill in the tube.

3. Hook the ruffles followed by the side petals (#4 and #5).

4. Hook the sepals (#6, #7, and #8). There are no ruffles in these areas.

Sarah Province hooked this lovely phalaeopsis orchid as part of *Mother's Garden.*

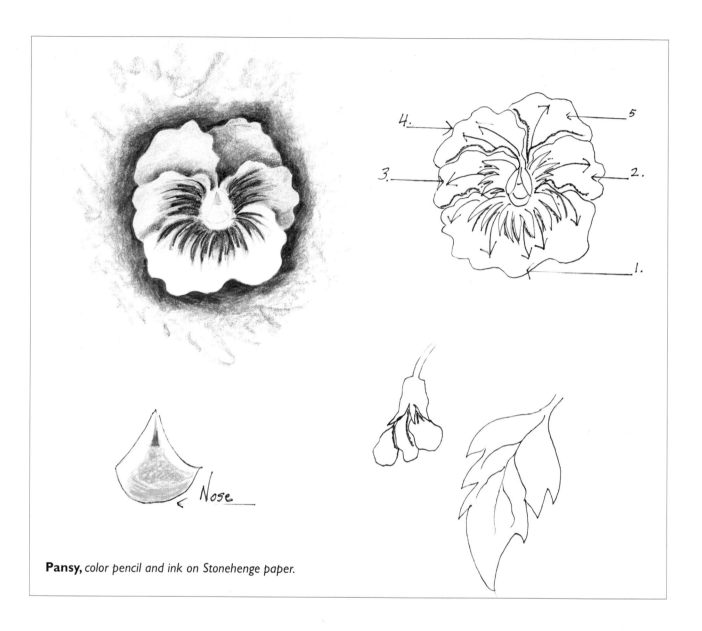

Pansy, *color pencil and ink on Stonehenge paper.*

Pansy (*Viola*)

> *"Take all the sweetness of a gift unsought,*
> *And for the pansies send me back a thought."*
> —Sarah Doudney

The name pansy is from the French word *pensee*, meaning thought or remembrance. Most weekend gardeners know the pansy as a delicate flower with a face. The pansy we know today did not exist before the mid-1800s. It was derived from a small wildflower known as a Johnny Jump Up or viola tricolor, and was cultivated over time into a specimen suitable for English gardens. Thus, the pansy arrived in America in 1848. This favorite with gardeners and artists is related to the simple blue violet.

Colors: The colors and color combinations are endless. Whatever your mind can imagine will be an acceptable color plan for a pansy. Yellow, violet, pink, blue, purple, red-violet, white, orange, hot pink, peach, red, and salmon are only a few of the possibilities. Black with a dot of yellow in the center seems like an unusual variety, but you can find it in flower catalogs.

Petals: The pansy has five rounded petals, and they appear in two familiar patterns. The first has a face with densely packed dark lines called *whiskers* emerging from the front three petals. The second pattern consists of lines radiating out from the center. These finer lines are called *penciling* and are similar to viola markings. The first type is hooked more frequently.

Flower center: This very special feature of the pansy is called the *nose*. The colors of the nose are white, chartreuse green, yellow, and orange. The whiskers or penciling are below the nose. Whiskers may be dark or light depending on the particular flower. Follow the diagram for detailed placement of color.

Mother's Garden, *detail. See full rug on page 124.*

Leaves and stems: The leaves are jagged and oval. The colors vary as in all leaves but the dominant green leans toward yellow.

Rating: 1

Challenge: Your challenges here will be squeezing all the colors into the nose and leaving just enough space between the whiskers to squeeze the petals' color in between these delicate whiskers.

Materials: One or two 6- to 8-value swatches. Beginners should limit themselves to one swatch. More advanced rug hookers can cross-swatch. Good cross-swatching combinations are purple and blue, red-violet and purple, or yellow and orange.

How to Hook

The entire flower (all five petals) can be hooked in all values of one color, or the front three petals can differ from the two back petals. More experienced rug hookers cross-swatch the entire flower by mingling two swatches together. Do this by separating the lighter values of two different swatches from the darker ones. The front petals can be hooked with the light shades and the back ones with the dark. It is not as common, but the reverse can also be effective.

It is perfectly acceptable for the whiskers to touch the edges of the two side petals. This positioning will make it easy to see the three front petals without having to add many shadows.

Curve the lines as you hook outward from the base of the petal to the edge. It is easiest to hook the sides of the petal to establish the curve and then hook toward the center, maintaining the curve.

1. This is a typical pansy with whiskers. Hook the nose first with a few loops. The touch of orange at the top of the nose is no more than one loop. If the flower is large, there may be more space to work with. Below the orange is chartreuse green, and below that is a row of yellow. Follow the diagram. Next are the whiskers. Make sure you leave space between the whiskers to slip in the petal color. The whiskers are uneven and curved.
2. Hook the front petal first. The value placed between the whiskers should be lighter than the whiskers themselves. Finger values from inside the whiskers to a light outside edge. If you are using a 6-value swatch, you might select the light and medium-light values for this front petal.
3. Continue hooking the side petals. Place the medium values inside the whiskers and hook out to a medium light edge.
4. The back petals are last. Use the dark values at the base of the petal and end with the medium value at the edge.
5. The buds are tightly wrapped petals. Hook the sepals, receptacle, and stem first. Hook light to dark. Your darkest value is just below the sepals. Make sure you can see that the underlying petals continue to get darker.

Sarah Province hooked this delightful miniature (*page 67*) of a group of pansies in her rug, *Mother's Garden*.

Sweet Pea (*Lathyrus*)

"Have you ever seen a flower down?
Sometimes angels skip around
And in their blissful state of glee
Bump into a daisy or sweet pea."
—Author unknown

A popular Victorian flower cultivated since the seventeenth century, the sweet pea originated in Sicily. This climbing plant has wonderful twisting stems and tendrils and is loved for its fragrance.

Colors: The color and color combinations are almost unlimited. Pink, lavender, white, cream, red, yellow, and blue are good choices.

Petals: This flower can look entirely different depending on its pose. The petals twist and turn and contain lots of ruffles. The plant is composed of a central pod, two petals on either side of the pod, and a larger petal in the back.

Leaves and stems: The leaves are small and oval with a wavy edge. The stems are hairy. The tendrils come out of the stem and provide a wonderful design element if you are drawing your own flowers. In the photograph of my *Sweet Pea (page 70)*, you can see that I took full advantage of the tendrils.

Rating: 6

Challenge: Creating the ruffles and capturing the delicacy of the flower are your two challenges.

Materials: 6- to 8-value swatch

How to Hook

If you can see the pod, always begin with it. The pod is the lightest part of the flower. Stay within the lines. This is a petite blossom, and expansion of the wool can make it look too large unless you are careful. Let's turn to the drawing:

A. This version of the flower is simple and slightly folded. The pod is the center and your lightest value. Hook this first. The two petals surrounding the pod are hooked second, followed by the back petal, which is the darkest of them all.
B. If you are a beginner, follow the lines in this drawing. Each petal is outlined and filled. You will need at least four values to hook this flower, including your lightest value in the pod, medium in the surrounding

Sweet Pea, *color pencil and ink on Canson paper.*

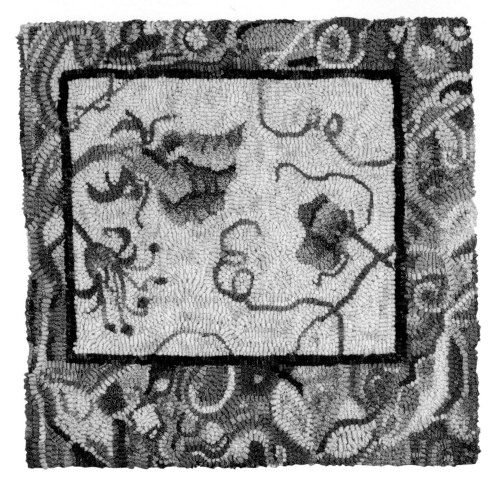

Sweet Pea, *13" x 13",*
#3- to 8-cut wool on cotton
warp cloth. Designed and
hooked by Jane Halliwell
Green, Edgewater, Maryland
2010.

petals, and dark for the back petal.

C. This version is more realistic. You will need, at minimum, a 6-value swatch. Since the petals are small, it can be difficult to finger the values with the exception of the back petal. Fill the pod with the tint. The surrounding petals are lighter at the edges. Surround the pod with the medium values and hook outward to medium light. In the back petal, work from your darkest value outward to a light edge. Be sure to curve your lines and stay inside the lines. Do not forget the ruffles: hook them one to two values darker.

D. This is an open pose. The pod is directly in the center. Note the shadow line in the middle of the pod and the many ruffles.

E. The three inner petals can be outlined and filled, and the back petal should be shaded from a dark base to a light edge.

F. The buds of a sweet pea have heads that hang down. Notice that the area under the sepals is dark.

G. This pose is more unusual. The back petal leans away from the pod and its surrounding petals. There is a turnover.

H. In this version of the sweet pea you have room to finger and shade the larger petals. The smaller ones can be filled. Be sure that the shadow under the petal's lip is dark enough. Hook the turnover

horizontally.

I. This shows the leaves and how they attach to the stem.

In *Sweet Pea*, I chose Color Family 11 for the noodle border which is orange, yellow-orange, yellow, yellow-green, and green. The entire outer edge is created with scraps in these closely related colors. The sweet pea is purple, which is the distant cousin of Family 11. For a description of this border, see Chapter 4. ☙

Primary Fusion #16
Use this dye formula to create
one of my favorite purples.
¹⁄₁₆ tsp. Magenta #338 (PC)
¹⁄₃₂ tsp. Blue #490 (PC)
¹⁄₆₄ tsp. Black #672 (PC)
Dissolve all three dyes in 1 c. of hot water.

Jane's Forget Me Not
This nice blue-violet is ideal
for a number of flowers.
¹⁄₄ tsp. Blue (C)
¹⁄₈ tsp. Lavender (C)
Dissolve both dyes in 1 c. of hot water.

CHAPTER TEN

Flower Shapes—Multiple Heads

> *"Silently, one by one, in the infinite meadows of heaven/*
> *Blossomed the lovely stars, the forget-me-nots of the angels."*
> —Henry Wadsworth Longfellow, "Evangeline"

Multiheaded flowers are clusters of many flowers that form a ball, cone, or other irregular shape. They look like a solid mass but are not. It is helpful to take a cluster apart to observe the individual flowers. With any flower cluster, the front blossoms are treated with more detail than those in the rear.

Forget-Me-Not (*Myosotis*)

This poem was written in the margins of a bill from Alaska, where the forget-me-not became the state flower:

> *"A little flower blossoms forth*
> *On every hill and dale*
> *The emblem of the Pioneers*
> *Upon the rugged trail.*
> *The Pioneers have asked it*
> *And we could deny them not;*
> *So the emblem of Alaska*
> *Is the blue Forget-me not."*

Thoreau described the forget-me-not as "small and unpretending—an interesting minute flower." Associated with many legends and considered the symbol of love, forget-me-nots are often chosen by brides for their bouquets.

Colors: Blue, pink, white, and lavender with blue are the most common colors, with some varieties having a pink streak down the center of the blue petal. In the open landscape thousands of forget-me-nots create carpets of blue.

Petals: The five simple flat petals have a circular outer shape.

Flower center: This is the interesting part. The center is slightly raised, bright yellow, with a tiny dot of dark green in the middle. A white area resembling a star

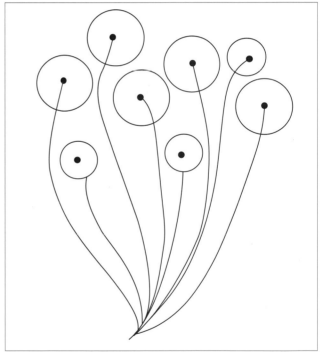

Geometric Representation of Multiheaded Flowers, *ink on Canson paper.*

surrounds the yellow and projects outward along the inner edges of the petals.

Leaves and stems: The stems are hairy with two or three flowers branching off. The leaves are elongated and smooth-edged with a crease down the center.

Rating: 1

Challenge: Choosing the correct combination of colors in the center is important because the center is the distinguishing characteristic.

Materials: This is a small flower and the petals do not overlap much, so two to four values will be sufficient to hook the petals.

Forget-me-nots, *color pencil and ink on Stonehenge paper.*

RIGHT: Oxford Gardens, *detail. See full rug on page 131.*

How to Hook

There is no order of hooking in this flower since the petals are relatively flat and have little overlap. Use Jane's Forget-Me-Not dye recipe (*page 70*) to create a unique color for this flower.

1. Start with the distinctive center. Study the colored drawing. To bring more attention to the center, sculpt the yellow area. Surround the yellow with white and carry the white out into the star shape.

2. Hook the top petal first followed by the remaining four petals. Squeeze dark values between the petals so you can see their separation. In a small flower like this, a few loops can be enough.

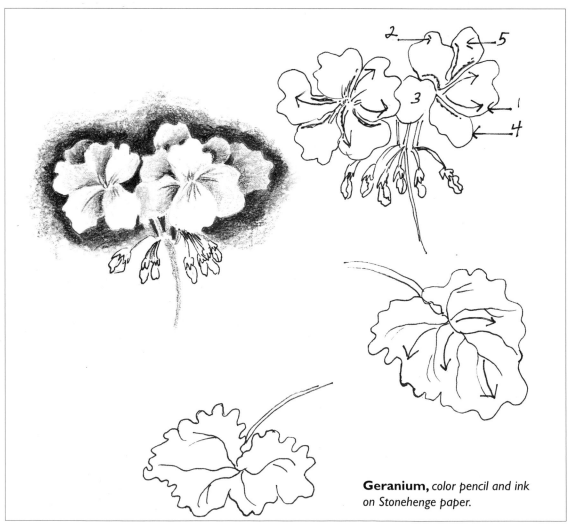

Geranium, *color pencil and ink on Stonehenge paper.*

Pelargonium's Geranium (*Pelargonium*)

Geraniums are popular container and hanging basket plants. The genus *Pelargonium* started as a South African herb. Since being transplanted from its native land, it has undergone many changes and is always referred to incorrectly as a geranium instead of a pelargonium. This delightful plant is often overlooked by rug hookers. The shapes of both the buds and the leaves make it an interesting flower for the artist.

Colors: Pink, red, orange, magenta, vermillion, and white with pink edges. Lavender and orange are available through garden supply catalogs.

Petals: There are five small petals. They have light veining, but the small size of the petals makes including the veins difficult. Numerous buds droop down beneath the full blossoms.

Leaves and stems: The fan-shaped leaves often have deep red or white variations, beautiful in their own right.

Flower center: Very small stamens and anthers emerge from the middle of the petal.

Rating: 4

Challenge: The biggest challenge is creating depth in a very small flower.

Materials: A spot dye with an added shadow, or a 2- to 4-value swatch

How to Hook

Because geraniums are so small, the easiest way to portray them is to proddy the blossoms. I used this technique to create the flowers in the wall hanging *Oxford Gardens*. Gene Shepherd is an expert on this technique.

Another simple approach is to fill each blossom with

Africa's Gift, *26" x 43", #3-cut wool on burlap.*
Designed by Jane McGown Flynn and hooked by Marion Thomson, Arlington, Virginia, 2010.

a spot dye such as Geranium and separate the petals with a dark blue or purple shadow color.

Marian Thomson hooked the exquisite rug *Africa's Gift* in a realistic manner. The finely shaded orange-red blossoms pop against the dark background. Marian balanced her colors by carrying over the flower's color to the leaf markings and geometric lines surrounding the outer edges of the rug.

If you use a 4-value swatch, the formula below will give you a true red.

WFS #26 Geranium

Dissolve ¼ tsp. Red (MC) in 1 cup of hot water, then use this formula to create values.

¼ tsp. Red #351 (PC)
dissolved in 1 c. hot water
¹⁄₁₂₈ tsp. Navy #413 (PC)
dissolved in 1 c. hot water
¹⁄₁₂₈ tsp. Yellow #119 (PC)
dissolved in 1 c. hot water
Spot 1 yard of natural, white, or pink wool. A darker version of this formula can be made by adding an additional ¼ teaspoon Red #351 and ¹⁄₆₄ teaspoon Navy #413.

Hydrangea (*Hydrangea*)

Sometimes described as snowballs, this flowering shrub is our grandmother's favorite flower. The color of its blossoms is determined by the acidity or alkalinity of the soil. Acid soils produce blue flowers, alkaline soils produce pink, and neutral soils bring out the whites. Hydrangeas are widely used as dried flowers.

Colors: Blue, pink, purple, white, cream, and pale yellow-green

Petals: There are four petals. The veins are shown in the shaded drawing; however, it is difficult to hook them because of their small size.

Bud: The bud looks like a little pie cut into slices.

Flower center: The flower center looks as though it contains tiny silver balls. A light center will not show up well so instead place one loop of a dark green or blue in the middle. Another strategy would be to use actual silver beads.

Leaves and stems: The hydrangea has large, heavily veined oval leaves with sawlike edges. The stems connect under the flower clusters and should be shown peeking out between the blossoms.

Rating: 5

Challenge: Make sure you manage the values correctly so that you have the appearance of many blossoms—light at the top and dark in the shadows.

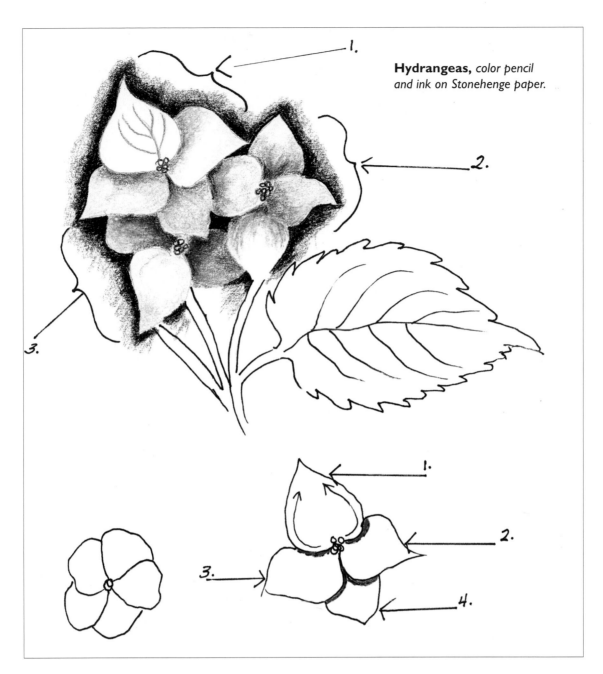

Hydrangeas, *color pencil and ink on Stonehenge paper.*

Materials: Working with two compatible 6- to 8-value swatches will expand the palette for a multitude of little blossoms. Good color combinations are pink with lavender, blue with lavender, and yellow-green with cream.

How to Hook

Follow this order when hooking the individual blossoms, starting with the top and working back into the shadows.

1. Hook the top, most fully exposed petals with the lightest values. Do not skip around. Complete all the light ones first. If you have two 6-value swatches, there will be four light values for the first layer.
2. Next, hook the flowers in the center using medium values.
3. Lastly, hook the dark spaces between the flowers using very dark materials. The actual shape of the darkest petals will not be evident. They will appear only as tiny irregular spaces between the light and medium values.
4. Stand back from the circular ball of individual flowers and squint. If the ball looks like a blob without any depth of value, you may need to rip out the medium values and replace them with a few darks.
5. Add the centers last by pixelating (two loops twisted like a French knot) or adding one dark bead.
6. Show the stems that connect the large balls together. The linear shapes of the stems up against the round balls make an interesting design statement.

Hydrangea, *28" x 43", #3- and 4-cut wool on linen. Designed by Jane McGown Flynn (#153) and hooked by Elissa Crouch, Cambridge, Maryland, 2010.*

Elissa Crouch hooked the sensational Jane McGown design *Hydrangea #153.* Elissa says she gazed at the pattern and the wool as they hung over a chair for a long time. Once she could imagine the rug in her mind, she began to work. She replaced the trellis on the outside border with various greens from the interior. ❧

CHAPTER ELEVEN

Flower Shapes—Rays, Pom-Poms, and Stars

"Art is the unceasing effort to compete with the beauty of flowers—and never succeeding."
—Gian Carlo Menotti

The flowers in this section sport petals radiating out from a central point and joining the stem in the middle. Viewed straight on, the blossoms are circular; but from an angle, they appear elliptical. The flowers in this section are often confused with each other. For example, asters and daisies look alike at first glance, but with careful inspection the aster resembles a sunflower. Color, shape, and size vary depending on the specimen.

If you sketch one of these plants, you will discover that the major challenge is portraying their overlapping petals. Selecting values to show the separation between petals is the first hurdle. Directional hooking within these small petals is another challenge.

Aster (*Aster*)

"We are the flower—Thou the Sun!
Forgive us, if as days decline-
We nearer steal to Thee!"
—Emily Dickinson

Asters are popular perennials found in North America. Also known as starworts, Michaelmas daisies, or frost flowers, they resemble chrysanthemums in many ways. Since a petal on an aster is almost never yellow, it is easily distinguished from a daisy or miniature sunflower.

Colors: White, red, pink, purple, lavender, blue, and red-violet

Petals: Asters have many overlapping spiky petals slightly narrower than a daisy's.

Flower centers: The center of an aster is called a *disk*. It is a collection of tiny tubular flowers grouped to-

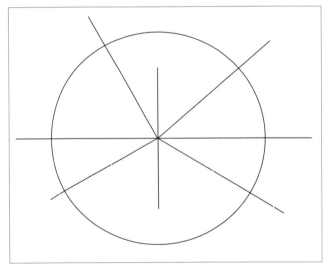

Geometric Representation of Rays, Pom-Poms, and Stars, *ink on Canson paper.*

gether and surrounded by ray flowers or petals. These tubular disk flowers can be a different color than the petals. The center is fluffy and slightly elevated. Its color is yellow-green, and it is encircled by gold or yellow bands.

Leaves and stems: The leaves are linear with ragged, rough edges.

Rating: 8

Challenge: The challenge is selecting values dark enough to see the individual petals.

Materials: 6- to 8-value swatch

Asters, *color pencil and ink on Stonehenge paper.*

How to Hook

1. If your fiber piece is a wall hanging, shag the center with a variety of yellow and gold strips. This technique will create the effect of a pom-pom.

2. Hook the top layer of petals first with tints and light values.

3. Hook the petals underneath the first layer with medium light and medium values.

4. The last layer of hidden petals is hooked with the darkest values.

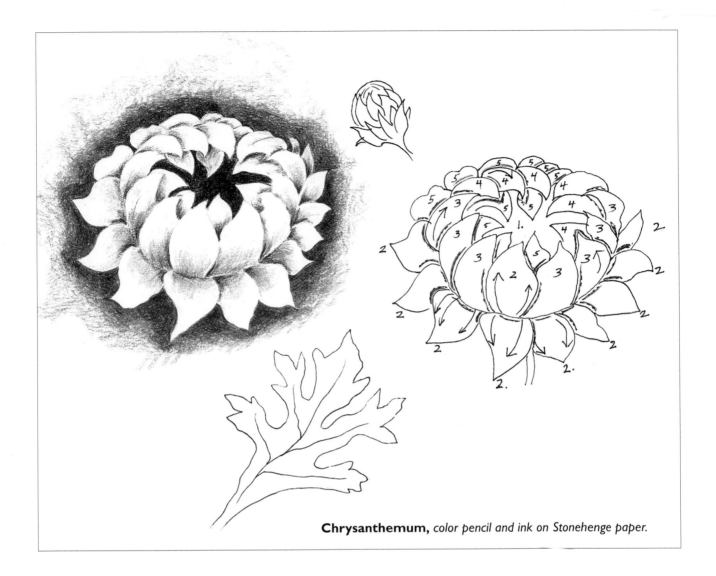

Chrysanthemum, *color pencil and ink on Stonehenge paper.*

Chrysanthemum (chrysanthemum)

Chrysanthemum comes from the Greek *chrysos*, meaning golden, and *anthos*, meaning flower. A huge variety of shapes from daisylike, decorative, pom-pom, or buttons in a wide range of colors and sizes are available. Cities in both China and Japan hold chrysanthemum festivals every year.

Colors: Yellow, white, purple-red, pink, rust, orange, and gold

Petals: Chrysanthemums have twenty or more overlapping petals ranging in width from 1" to 4" across.

Flower center: The center is the largest open space. The darkest value belongs here.

Leaves and stems: The leaves are large, linear, and lobed.

Rating: 10++

Challenge: Choosing values that are dark enough to see the numerous overlapping petals is the challenge.

Materials: Cross-swatch two or more 6- to 8-value swatch sets.

How to Hook

Choose a larger chrysanthemum when hooking this flower for the first time.

1. Start with the center. Outline and fill this distinct middle shape with your deepest and darkest value. Everything else in the flower will be lighter.

2. Proceed to the outer ring of petals and find the petal on top, or rather, the petal seen in its entirety. For this first layer choose tint to light values. Hook one petal at a time and do not rush. Add darker values between the petals and skip values when necessary.

3. Continue to the second ring, and do the same. The second ring will have the medium to dark values.

4. In the last ring closest to the dark center, return to the lighter values. There should be a fair amount of contrast between these upper petals and the dark interior.

Julie Gibson's chrysanthemum (*page 80*), which is a part of a larger flower sampler, illustrates this step-by-step placement of values along with the important contrast in the center.

White Flower Sampler, *#3-cut wool on linen.*
Designed by Jane McGown Flynn and hooked by Julie Gibson, Tucson, Arizona, 2009. JULIE GIBSON

Clematis TRUDY SIMMONS

Clematis, *color pencil and ink on Stonehenge paper.*

Clematis (*Clematis*)

> *"Thrive, gentle plant!*
> *And weave a bower for Mary and me,*
> *And deck with many a splendid flower*
> *thy foliage large and free."*
> —William Cowper, 1765

Clematis belongs to the same family as the buttercup. Travelers in the American Old West called this plant "pepper vine" because it was used to spice up food when true black pepper was too costly. Clematis is the queen of climbers.

Colors: Almost an unlimited number of color combinations depending on the particular variety.

Petals: The petal edges are ruffled like the scalloped edge of a child's dress. There is a distinct crease down the center. This crease is a double line and extends the length of the petal from the center to the petal tip. The plant can have as few as four to as many as twenty petals in a diameter of 1" to 8" across. Each petal ends in a point.

Flower center: The center is the distinguishing characteristic of the clematis. In the illustration, you can see a small center with bulging sides. The color of the center is usually gold surrounded by numerous long, white, stringy stamens.

Leaves and stems: The plant boasts woody stems and leaves that twist and curl around fences and arbors as it grows. The leaves are oval with smooth edges.

Rating: 2

Challenge: The double creases down the center of the petals require the selection of the correct values.

Materials: 4- to 8-value swatch

How to Hook

Start with the petals and leave the center for last.

1. Hook the creases down the center of the petal first. These creases are side-by-side lines with room for at least one row of petal color in between. Choose one value darker than the petal.

2. To simplify the flower, select one value to fill each petal. Hook lengthwise. For greater detail, hook each petal with two values. Start with the top (lightest) petal and finish with the underlying dark ones.

3. The flower center is the fun part. Sculpt the round area in the middle of the center, and surround it with shagging or yarn and embroidery thread tied to the reverse side.

Cosmos, *color pencil and ink on Stonehenge paper.*

Cosmos (*Cosmos*)

The word *cosmos* is derived from the Greek word *kosmos*, meaning order and ornament. The flower lives up to its description, appearing very balanced. The petals come off the central disk, are broader than asters and daisies, and are slightly overlapped.

Colors: White, pink, orange, yellow, and scarlet

Petals: The petals are 8" to 10" long and overlapping, but they are not as densely packed as asters and chrysanthemums. They possess numerous creases and uneven tips.

Flower center: The center is yellow and gold. The band around the center may be surrounded with a darker value of the flower's color.

Leaves: The leaves are smooth, squiggly, and bright.

Rating: 1

Challenge: Choosing the right values to depict the creases down the length of the petal is the challenge.

Materials: 4-value swatch

How to Hook

This is an easy flower because there is little overlap between the petals.

1. Begin the textured center with tweed over dyed with yellow. Make the half-moon very dark.

2. Hook the petals lengthwise. Each petal can contain a different value. Hook the creases first, one value darker than the petal.

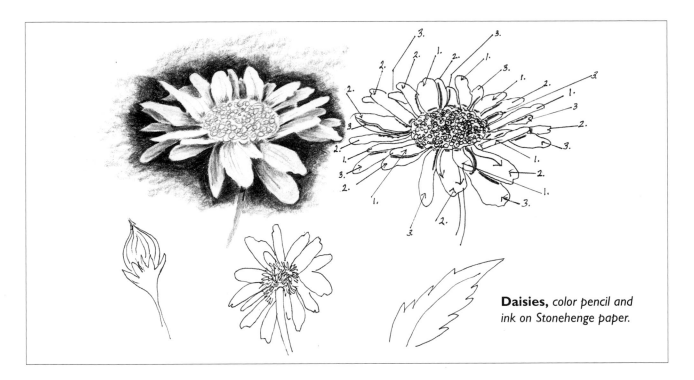

Daisies, *color pencil and ink on Stonehenge paper.*

Daisy (*Bellis*)

"Stoop where thou wilt,
thy careless hand some random bud will meet;
Thou canst not tread, but thou wilt find
The Daisy at thy feet."
—Thomas Hood, Song

Songs and poems have been dedicated to this simple and sophisticated flower for centuries. An artists' favorite, daisies symbolize new beginnings and loyal love. There are numerous varieties, including Gerbera daisies, blue daisies, sunshine daisies, and gloriosas (coneflowers). Daisies make us smile, and perhaps this is why they pop up in our rugs again and again. Black-eyed Susans and coneflowers are part of the same family. The black-eyed Susan is similar to a daisy except that the center is a golden brown and the petals gold. The coneflower has a center that protrudes upward while the petals fall downward.

Colors: White, yellow, rust, gold, salmon, pink, and red

Petals: Daisies have overlapping petals with a tiny indentation at the tip. There are indentations down the center, but because of the narrowness of the petal, these creases can be omitted.

Flower center: Like the aster, the central disk is composed of many tiny tubular florets. A small circular area in the middle of the center is yellow-green. The remaining disk is yellow or gold. The center looks like a puffy pin cushion. Consider sculpting the center with tweed. The edge is a good place to slip in another color from another flower in the rug.

Leaves and stems: The leaves are narrow, feather-like, and ragged.

Rating: 1

Challenge: Work hard to capture the shadows on the underlying petals.

Materials: 4- to 8-value swatch

How to Hook

Both primitive and fine-shaded versions require hooking the center first. A textured material belongs in the center. Surround the center with color carried from another flower.

Primitive approach:
1. Hook the top petals first. These are labeled #1 in the drawing. Use the lightest value and hook along the length of the petal.
2. Hook the #2 petals in a medium value.
3. Hook the #3 petals last using the darkest values.

Finely shaded approach:
1. Follow the directions above but add additional values.
2. The #1 petals should be hooked with a tint to a light value.
3. The #2 petals will be hooked in a medium to medium dark value.
4. Hook the #3 petals last with dark to very dark hues.
5. Always evaluate the final results to determine if a darker shadow is needed between two petals.

   Tip: Consider drawing a design that includes the back side of a daisy.

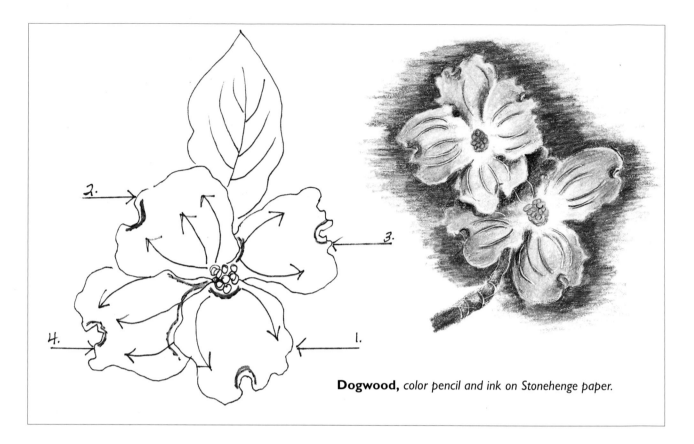

Dogwood, *color pencil and ink on Stonehenge paper.*

Dogwood (*Cornus*)

The dogwood tree is a familiar sign of spring. Its blossom is the state flower of Virginia, and it is a simple flower to hook.

Colors: Pale bronze green to white, pink, and rose

Petals: The flower contains four petals. At the end of the petal is a small green or reddish brown notch. There are distinct creases in the petal and hooking both the crease and the notch is important because these are distinguishing characteristics.

Flower center: The center resembles yellow beads surrounded by a dark green circle. Pixelate this area with yellow-green tweed to replicate seeds.

Leaves and stems: Leaves are wavy, smooth, and oval.

Rating: 1. This is a good flower for beginners.

Challenge: You'll face two challenges with this flower: capturing the creases in the petal and making sure the notch at the tip of the petal does not disappear into the background.

Materials: 4- to 8-value swatch

How to Hook

Hook a dark line of green under the center to better define it. I call this the *smile*. Pixelate this area with green and yellow tweed. If the work is a wall hanging, try adding beads in the center instead of hooking regular loops. Create the notches with a tail/loop/tail of reddish brown or olive green.

Primitive approach: Using a 4-value swatch, outline each petal and fill it in with a different value. Capture the shape of the petal, notch, and center seeds. Omit the detail of the petal creases.

Finely shaded approach: Hook the creases in the petals. Do one at a time, as the value of the crease will change as your petal gets progressively darker. All lines lead to the notch at the end of the petal. Using a 6- to 8-value swatch, shade the top petal first. Most dogwood blossoms are lighter near the center and darker at the edges.

Use the Fig dye recipe (*page 47*) which leans green and is an excellent choice for this flower.

Build a gradation with the following formulas:
¼ tsp. Taupe (C) dissolved in 1 c. hot water
(Taupe leans lavender.)
¼ tsp. #672 Black (PC)
dissolved in 1 c. hot water
¼ tsp. Aqualon yellow (C)
dissolved in 1 c. hot water
¼ tsp. Aqualon pink (C)
dissolved in 1 c. hot water
¼ tsp. Old Ivory (C)
dissolved in 1 c. hot water

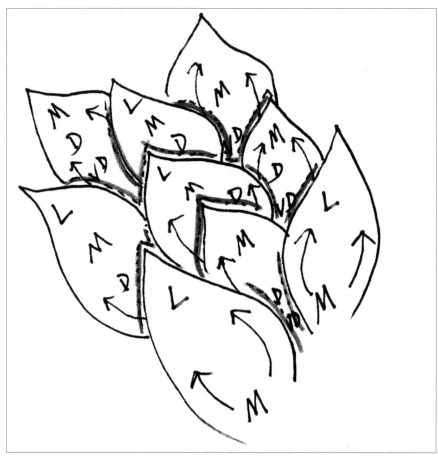

Section of a Night-Blooming Cereus, *ink on Stonehenge paper.*

Night-Blooming Cereus Cactus (*Peruvianus monstrosus*)

The night-blooming cereus is a Mexican cactus. The petals are thin, pointed, and grow out of the rounded tips of the cactus. The spectacular flower is short-lived: the blossoms start opening just after dark and are fully opened several hours later. At dawn's first light, they start to wilt and are gone forever. The Chinese will not marry when this flower is blooming because its short bloom is regarded as a bad omen.

The cereus is rarely hooked. Add this to your list as a new flower to try. The flower offers opportunities to use new techniques, such as creating the flower center or the prickles on the cactus.

Margaret Grabus hooked a magnificent single night-blooming cactus. She used embroidery thread and beads in the center. Gold beads were repeated in the background. One loop of embroidery thread created the spikes on the cactus.

Use White Magic (*page 46*) to dye wool for this flower.

Color: Bronze-green, white, or gray
Petals: The petals are sharp and pointed.
Flower center: A multitude of stringy and delicate stamens and anthers emerge out of a yellow-green center.

Leaves and stems: The yellow-green cactus is rounded at the top and covered with sharp points. Margaret used thread that was knotted and cut to depict these points.

Rating: 7
Challenge: The challenges here are the placement of dark values in a flower with many overlapping petals.
Materials: 8-value white swatch

How to Hook

If you hook the flower as a wall hanging, start with the petals and not the center.

1. The petals closest to the center are the lightest ones. Begin here with pure white and tints.
2. Hook the next layer of petals a little farther from the center. At the base of the petal where they touch the first row, use dark values.
3. Proceed to the next layer, always placing progressively darker values at the base of the petal.
4. Margaret shagged the center with her woolen fabric. This raised the center so that it stood out above the surrounding embroidery thread.

Night-Blooming Cereus, *13" x 17", #3-cut wool, embroidery thread, and beads on cotton warp cloth. Designed by Jane Halliwell Green and hooked by Margaret Grabus, Stevensville, Maryland, 2010.*

Center of **Night-Blooming Cereus,** *above.*

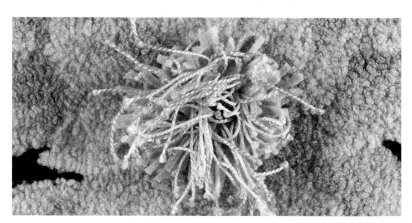

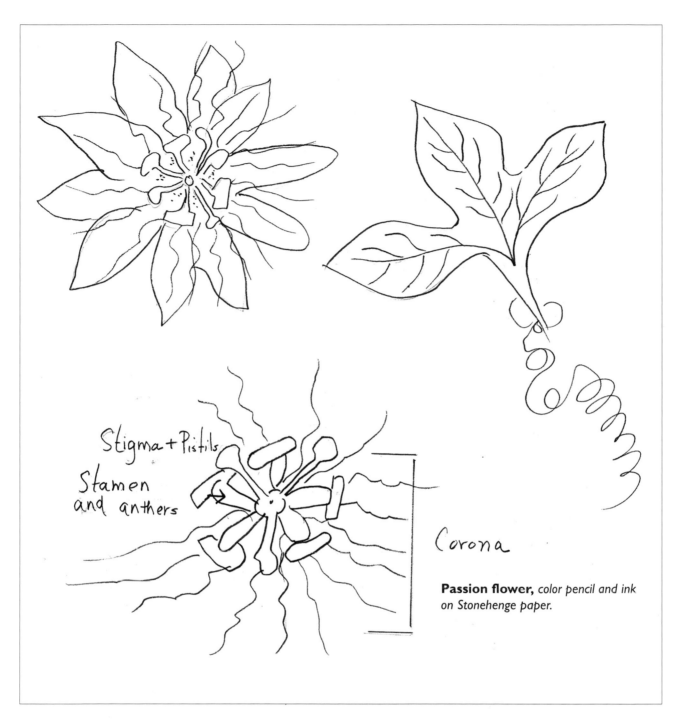

Stigma + Pistils

Stamen
and anthers

Corona

Passion flower, *color pencil and ink on Stonehenge paper.*

Passion Flower (*Passiflora*)

"My love gave me a passion-flower.
I nursed it well—so brief its hour!
My eyelids ache, my throat is dry:
He told me that I would not die."
　　　　　—Margaret Fuller

This fast-growing vine, named by Spanish explorers who saw religious symbolism in the plant, is native to Brazil and Argentina. They compared the ten sepals to the ten apostles present at the crucifixion of Christ, and the five stamens to the five wounds. The flower has a high medicinal value as a mild sedative and antianxiety drug. It can be purchased in an organic green grocer. It is also called passion vine and maypop.

Use PF #16 (*page 70*), White Magic (*page 46*), and Fig (*page 47*) to dye wool for this flower.

Colors: White, purple, and red are the common colors associated with this flower.

Petals: Although the passion flower appears to have ten petals beneath the corona, there are actually only five. The remaining five are sepals. The petals and sepals are not always the same color.

Flower center: The center is complicated. Because

Mammoth Passion Flower, *16" x 16", #8-cut wool on linen. Designed by Fraser Rugs and hooked by Helen Vance, Reston, Virginia, 2009.*

its center is the distinguishing characteristic of the flower, it helps to break down the parts:

- There are three pistils with stigmas at the top. They are often purple.
- There are five stamens, which are yellow-green and yellow. The anthers and filaments are part of these five projections.
- The corona is the ring of spiky petal-like structures. The common passion vines have multicolored coronas that are dark purple toward the center with tips that create a ring of white and bluish lavender. In other varieties it might be solid purple, white, blue, red, or mottled. The corona can emerge straight out

from the center, or the petal-like projections may instead twist and turn, looking just like angel hair pasta.

- Underneath all these parts are distinctive dots or speckles in a contrasting color.

Leaves and stems: The leaves are triangular, lobed, and shiny. At their base, the tendrils twist and turn tightly numerous times.

Rating: 9

Challenge: Capturing the detail in the fascinating center is difficult.

Materials: Dip dyes or swatch

Mammoth Passion Flower, *16" x 16", #8-cut wool on linen. Designed by Fraser Rugs and hooked by Carol Fields Hagen, Centreville, Virginia, 2009.*

How to Hook

Refer to the diagram of the flower and flower center. Because shading is not so important in this flower, only an ink rendition is shown.

1. Tackle the center first by hooking the purple pistils and stamens.
2. Surround the center with a material in a contrasting color. Red-violet is a good choice.
3. Hook the corona in a lighter or darker color than the petals and sepals. ***Note: If you decide to capture the corona with threads or yarn, hook it last.***
4. There is minimal shading in hooking the sepals and petals, which barely overlap. Four values of a swatch

can be rotated around the circle, filling each petal and sepal with a different one.

Helen Vance and Carol Fields Hagen took my workshop, called "Close-Ups," to learn how to hook wide-cut flowers. Helen and Carol took this very complicated flower, rarely rendered in fiber, and simplified it to create an elegant piece of art. Both chose unusual backgrounds: Helen a dark green spot dye hooked in circles, and Carol a spot dye with soft pink tones. I was thrilled to see the final results.

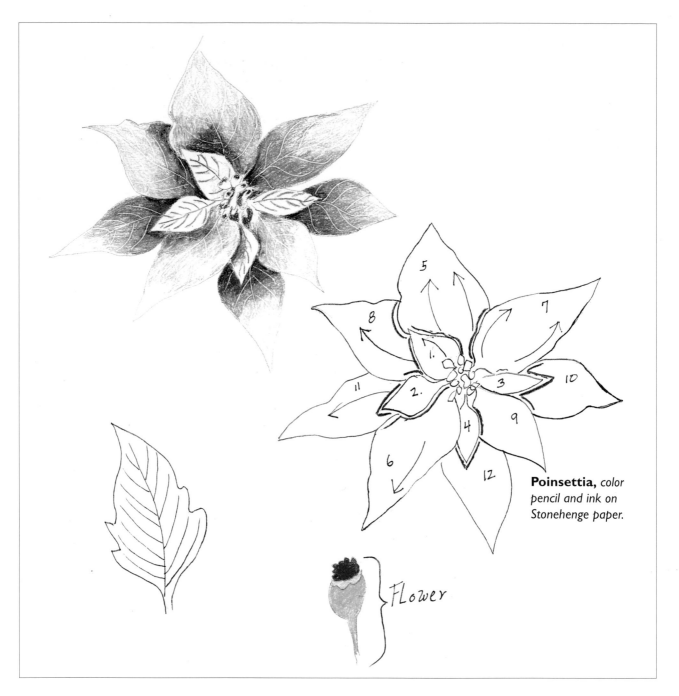

Poinsettia, *color pencil and ink on Stonehenge paper.*

Flower

Poinsettia (*Euphorbia pulcherrima*)

Poinsettias are native to Mexico. The ancient Aztecs prized the plant as a symbol of purity and used the leaves to make purple dyes. Most people think the brightly colored red leaves are flowers, when actually the real flowers are the small yellow berries in the center. The showy part of the plant is the red bracts that are often confused with the leaves. Poinsettias in the house during the Christmas season is a tradition in most families.

Colors: White, red, and pink. Three-quarters of Americans still prefer red poinsettias.

Petals: None. Instead, what looks like a petal is really a bract. Bracts are specialized leaves that look like petals.

They are smaller on the inside, and gradually get longer toward the outside of the plant.

Flower center: Yellow-green, red, and yellow "seeds" or "berries" appear in the center. These are actually the flowers of the plant. Pixelate, loop shag, or add beads to decorate the center.

Leaves and stems: The stems are thick. The long, oval-shaped leaves have prominent veins, which are lighter than the color of the leaf. The leaves come to a sharp point.

Rating: 6

Challenge: First, a true red flower can be challenging because lighter values of a red swatch can be pink or orange. Second, the layers containing the bracts are not

Poinsettia #1, *11" x 9", #4-cut wool on burlap. Designed and hooked by Ingrid Hieronimus, Petersburg, Ontario, Canada, 1999.* INGRID HIERONIMUS

perfectly circular so determining the placement of values requires a careful assessment of the position of a particular bract in relation to the others.

    Materials: 8-value swatch or dip dye

How to Hook

Save the center, which contains the actual flowers, until last if you intend to use beads instead of regular loops.

1. Start with the small bracts near the center of the flower. The prominent veins require a value slightly darker than the petal color.

2. After completing the small top bracts, determine which bracts are more exposed and hook them in the middle values. Proceed to hook the bracts further from the center and underneath the top bracts with darkest values.

    Ingrid Hieronimus shows a good way to approach a poinsettia. In *Poinsettia 1*, she uses two different dip dyes to hook the petals. In a simpler approach, the exterior of the petal could be outlined with a red dip dye and filled with Dorr's natural wool.

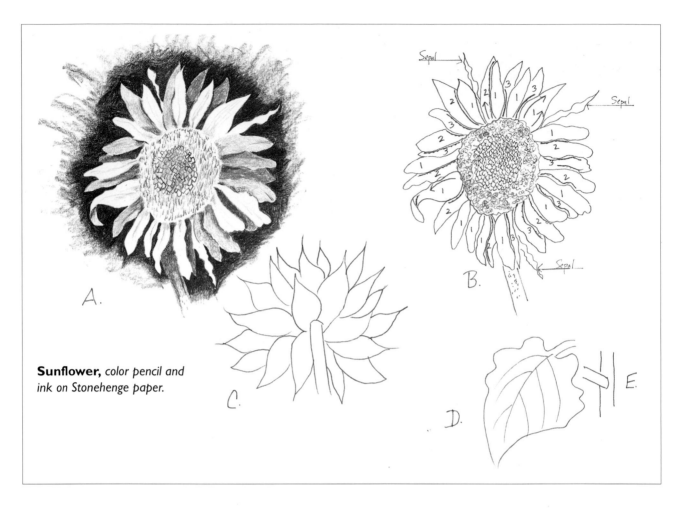

Sunflower, *color pencil and ink on Stonehenge paper.*

A.

B.

C.

D.

E.

Sepal

Sunflower (*Helianthus*)

Could this be the most popular flower in the rug hooking world? Today it is, but to my surprise, little evidence can be found of its popularity during the 1940s to 1980s. It has been sculpted, prodded, and hooked a million different ways. Anyone who has traveled to Italy and marveled at the miles of sunflowers will understand the power this flower has over the artist.

The botanical name, *helianthus*, is derived from *helios* (sun) and *anthos* (flower). The domestication of the sunflower dates back to 1000 BC.

The size of the flower is often a foot in diameter. According to the *Guinness Book of World Records*, the tallest sunflower ever measured towered over 25 feet.

Colors: Yellow-gold, maroon, and orange

Petals: Two rows of overlapping petals.

Flower center: The dramatic center is called the *head* and is composed of numerous flowers tightly packed together. Centers may vary—some are composed of a single ring and others two. Yellow, brown, yellow-green, purple, gold, and combinations of these colors are possibilities. Try high and low hooking in the middle, setting the loops lower in the center and higher in the outer rings. Try the techniques of shagging, loop shagging, and sculpting. When the design includes multiple flowers, vary the centers. Jo Ann Hendrix's rug is an excellent example.

Leaves and stems: The stalk is thick and hairy with large, smooth-edged, heart-shaped leaves. The sepals on the back of the flower are often as interesting as the front, which is why artists often show at least one flower turned backward.

Rating: 2

Challenge: Because the petals and sepals share a similar shape, the challenge is distinguishing between them.

Materials: If the flower is large enough, select a dip dye with additional darks for the shadows. Casseroles are also a good choice. Use a swatch for smaller sunflowers. For a close-up version, a dip dye is the best choice. Kathy Meentemeyer hooked her dramatic sunflower (*page 94*) with twisting petals using ripped 1" strips.

How to Hook

The illustration includes the following:

🌿 The shaded drawing (A)

🌿 Directional hooking and order of hooking with #1 representing the first and lightest petals, #2 the middle values, and #3 the last and darkest ones (B)

Sunflower Rug, *23" x 42½", #6- to 8-cut wool on linen. Designed by Kim Nixon and hooked by Jo Ann Hendrix, Pasadena, Maryland, 2010.*

Giant Sunflower, *42" x 42", ripped strips of wool on linen. Designed by Jane Halliwell Green and hooked by Kathy Meentemeyer, St. Louis, Missouri, 2001.* KATHY MEENTEMEYER

- The back of the flower showing the numerous sepals (C)
- The heart-shaped leaf (D)
- The manner in which the stem attaches to the stalk (E)

Use two different fabrics for the center. Even a single brown center needs a change in tone and value. The study of a sunflower reveals an almost geometric or diamond-shaped inner ring surrounded by a shaggier exterior ring. Jo Ann Hendrix cleverly played up this feature in one of her sunflower's centers.

Follow the illustration for placement of values. Hook the petals lengthwise.

TC #1

This is a three-color casserole.
My standard size wool is 10" x 15" to fit my pan. If you prefer the greater length to be yellow, make the red and orange parts shorter as you spoon the colors onto the fabric.
⅛ tsp. Magenta #338 (PC)
dissolved in 1 c. hot water
⅛ tsp. Orange #233 (PC)
dissolved in 1 c. hot water
⅛ tsp. Yellow #119 (PC)
dissolved in 1 c. hot water

Sunflower Rug, *detail. See full on page 93.*

TC #2
This is a two-color casserole.
⅛ tsp. Orange #233 (PC)
dissolved in 1 c. hot water
⅛ tsp. Yellow #119 (PC)
dissolved in 1 c. hot water

Primary Fusion #42
This formula makes a bright sunflower.
⅛ tsp. yellow #119 (PC)
1/128 tsp. Magenta #338 (PC)
Dissolve dyes in 1 c. of hot water.

PR9
Gold Nugget from Prisms 2 is a soft gold.
¼ tsp. #119 (PC)
1/16 tsp. Fuchsia #349 (PC)
1/32 tsp. Black #672 (PC)
Dissolve dyes in 1 c. of hot water.

Use Everything Spot (*page 49*) for a great addition to a Sunflower center.

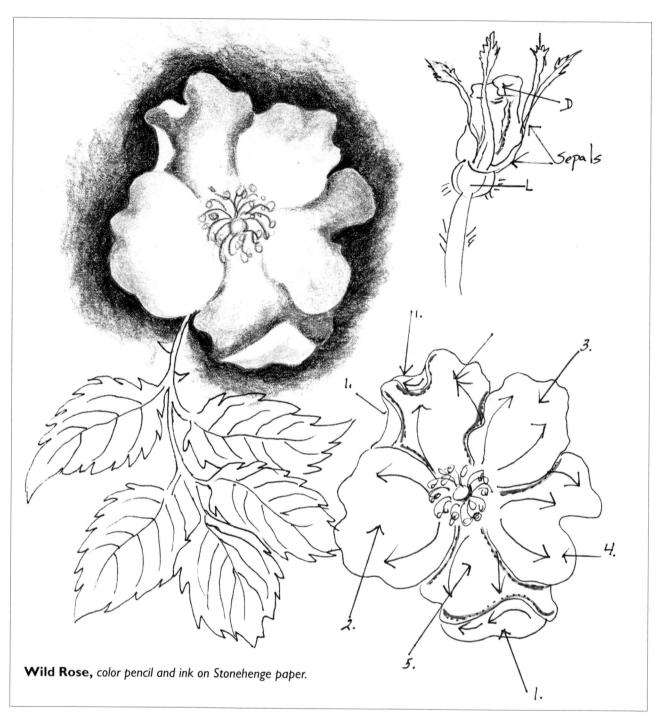

Wild Rose, *color pencil and ink on Stonehenge paper.*

Wild Species Rose (*Rosa*) or Old Rose

"What's in a name? That which we call a rose
By any other name would smell as sweet."
—William Shakespeare

Unlike its cousin the tea rose, the wild rose is a relatively simple flower with an interesting and busy center. A wild rose is a good choice for a new rug hooker.

Colors: Pink, yellow, salmon, white, and red

Petals: Five or more petals depending on the variety. There is often a dip in the outer edge.

Bud: The bottom edge of the bud is surrounded by sepals that end in a point.

Flower center: A yellow-green circle is often surrounded by a circular cascade of yellow stamens tipped off with yellow anthers.

Leaves and stems: The leaves are oval with sawlike edges.

Rating: 2

Challenge: The center is the distinguishing characteristic. Try hooking it with threads or yarn.

Materials: 4- to 6-value swatch. If the flower is large enough, a short dip dye may work well.

Wild Rose and Petunia *(finished as a footstool), 14" round, #3-cut wool on cotton rug warp.*
Designed by Jane McGown Flynn (CS 544) and hooked by Jeanne Sullivan, Annapolis, Maryland.

How to Hook

1. Place the circular dot of green in the center. If you have a large enough flower, sculpt this part.

2. If you plan to use thread for the many stamens that circle the central spot, save this part for last and hook the light turnovers next. Turnovers are hooked in slightly curved horizontal lines. Under each hook a single line of dark shadow.

3. Continue to the first and lightest petal, working from the base to the outer edge and from the sides toward the center. Pay special attention to the shadows between the petals.

4. When the petals are complete, sew threads or yarn around the middle disk of the plant.

Jeanne Sullivan hooked a beautiful piece entitled *Wild Rose and Petunia*. The turnovers are handled perfectly, with just enough dark shadow under the lip. The color of the wild roses was carried in the veins of the leaves. ☙

CHAPTER TWELVE

Flower Shapes—Spikes

"The flowers take the tears of weeping night, and give them to the sun for the days delight."
—Gian Carlo Menotti

Spikes are composed of small flowers surrounding a central stem. Think of them as inverted cones: narrow at the top and wide at the bottom. They can be hooked as one shape in an impressionistic manner, or the individual flowers can be treated separately. As you climb up the stem the flowers become smaller. Unopened buds sit on top.

Gladiolus (*Gladiolus*)

"A flower is relatively small. Still in a way, nobody sees a flower, so I said to myself, I'll paint it big."
—Georgia O'Keefe

The gladiolus flower, also known as a sword lily, comes from the ancient Greek word *gladius*, meaning sword. The blossoms are either plain, trumpet-shaped forms or the common frilled variety that resemble butterflies. The flower is rarely tackled by rug hookers, which is unfortunate because of the wide variety of colors it affords us.

Colors: White, yellow, pink, lavender, red, and red-violet. The color palette is almost unlimited.

Petals: There are six petals. The blossoms are flamboyantly ruffled as they cling to the hearty stalk. The ruffles can extend right up to the center of the flower or lie gently on the edge. The buds look like arrows as they protrude outward from the sides and top of the stalk.

Flower center: The stamens and anthers are clearly seen as they grow out of the center smile. The area inside the smile is dark, and its color is dependent upon the specimen. A visual aid is helpful with this plant.

Leaves and stems: The sword-shaped leaves are narrow with smooth edges ending in a sharp point.

Rating: 8. Large flowers are easier to hook.

Challenge: The creases and ruffles are important

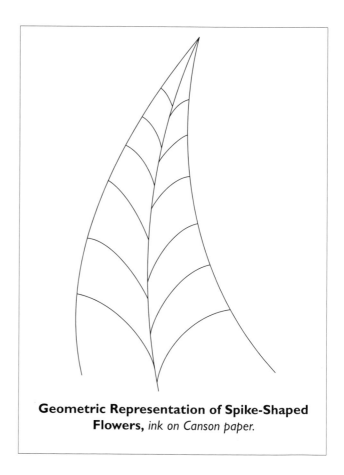

Geometric Representation of Spike-Shaped Flowers, *ink on Canson paper.*

features of gladiolas and are one of the challenges. The second challenge is keeping track of values where blossoms overlap and appear to merge together.

Materials: Tassey Mariani's rug (*page 100*) is hooked with two 8-value swatches. A dip dye will not provide the wide range of values available in a gradation. The choice depends on the size of the flower and the amount of detail desired by the artist. Tassey chose to hook an enlarged flower instead of the entire stalk.

2

5

1

6

Highlight

Highlight

3

4

7

Gladiolus, *color pencil and ink on Stonehenge paper.*

Close-Up Gladiolus, *44" x 42", #8-cut and hand-ripped wool on linen. Designed by Jane Halliwell Green and hooked by Tassey Mariani, Darnestown, Maryland, 2011.*

How to Hook

1. There is a smile in the area just below the stamens in the flower's center. Hook the smile in a dark value first.
2. Hook the stamens and anthers in the color of your chosen specimen. Yellow-green stamens and maroon anthers are common center colors. This flower may be hooked from a light interior out to a dark edge, or vice versa. Your background color will determine this.
3. In a rug showing a full spike, hook the top and lightest flower first and work downward toward the base of the stalk.
4. Each blossom contains six petals. The shadows in the ruffles should be hooked first. It is unnecessary to include ruffles on every blossom; hook a few and your audience will imagine the remainder.
5. Hook the lightest value in the most exposed petal.
6. Continue to work toward the darkest parts of the flower at the bottom.

To Dye Tassey's Gladiolus

Each dye formula yielded eight values. Each piece of wool was ⅙ of a yard. The gradation was started with 1 tablespoon and doubled all the way to the darkest value. The swatches are close in color and can be cross-swatched.

Gladiolus #1
¼ tsp. Blue (MC) and ¼ tsp. Blue-Violet (MC)
dissolved in 2 c. water

Gladiolus #2
¼ tsp. Blue (MC) and ¼ tsp Red-Violet (MC)
dissolved in 2 c. water

Hollyhock, *color pencil and ink on Stonehenge paper.*

Hollyhock (*Alcea*)

The hollyhock is related to the hibiscus, but unlike the hibiscus, which is a shrub, hollyhocks produce multiple blooms on a central stem. The plant can grow as tall as 9' and looks gorgeous against buildings and fences. It is a common perennial in English cottage gardens. The plant's botanical name, *Alcea*, is derived from the Greek word *althea*, which means to cure. Hollyhocks possess medicinal properties and were used by the Chinese to treat earaches and toothaches.

Colors: Yellow, pink, white, mauve, red, and white

Petals: The blossoms are large and ruffled along the edges and appear to weigh the stalk down. There is distinct veining. Buds are prominent and perch on top of the stalk.

Flower centers: The center is a cone-shaped anther heavy with pollen. It is white, yellow-green, or a darker version of the petal's color.

Leaves and stems: The leaves of the hollyhock are large, multi-veined, and lobed. The stalk is thick and tall.

Oxford Gardens, *detail. See full rug on page 131.*

Rating: 3

Challenge: Hooking the ruffles is the hardest part of this flower.

Materials: Dip dyes plus an additional color for the veins and shadows are necessary. Spot dyes may be a good choice for a vein but watch out for bright colors.

How to Hook

1. Because the flower is relatively flat, it is a good choice for a new rug hooker. The order of hooking is not shown on the drawing because one hooks from the inside of the flower out toward the edge. The shadows between the petals are less important than the ruffles and creases.

2. Start with the center. Since the center of the hollyhock is very fluffy, sculpt this part.

3. Most hollyhock varieties are dark around the center and become light at the edges. In a large flower, hook the ruffles before the petals. In *Oxford Gardens,* the hollyhocks were small so only a few ruffles were added at the petal's edge. Choose a fabric in a medium value for the ruffles and do not worry if some of the ruffle disappears. The goal is to imply that the ruffles are there, not to make them too bold.

4. Where one petal lies over another, be sure to shadow the overlap.

Pink Hollyhock

This is how I dyed the hollyhocks in *Oxford Gardens.* The center was sculpted with white wool slightly tinted with pink. The flowers are dip dyed using wool cut into 9" x 13" pieces.

¼ tsp. Cherry (C) dissolved in 1 c. hot water
1/32 tsp. Rose (C) dissolved in 1 c. hot water

Place about ¼ cup of dye in two separate pans and include the vinegar. Control the lightness or darkness of either side of the dip by adding less or more of the formulas to the pan.

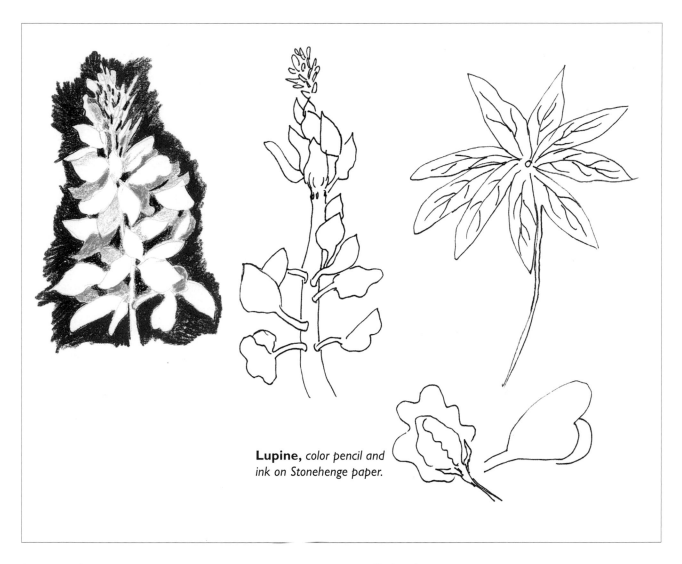

Lupine, *color pencil and ink on Stonehenge paper.*

Lupine (*Lupinus*)

This dramatic plant is well known in New England. In fact, the lupine is to Maine what the bluebell is to Texas! It is a tall flower and a member of the pea family. Like sunflowers, lupines fill fields with color.

The lupine drawing shows the shape of the petal, a close up of the top of the stalk, and the way stems grow from it.

Colors: Deep blue, purple, red-violet, and creamy yellow

Petals: The petals are almost exactly like a miniature version of the sweet pea growing in the shape of a spike. Each blossom consists of an upper standard or banner, two lateral wings, and two lower petals fused as a keel. There is a distinct spike at the top.

Leaves and stems: The narrow leaves form a circle and originate out of a yellow central point. Play up these unusually shaped leaves. The stalk is wide and peeks out between the flowers as your eyes move up the stalk. The stems grow directly out of the stalk.

Rating: 4

Challenge: Your challenge is to capture the essence of this flower without hooking excessive detail.

Materials: Three values: light, medium, and dark

How to Hook

1. You can suggest a lupine without overworking the details. If you capture the spike-like shape, your job is halfway finished.
2. Hook the parts of the stem that are visible and not covered by leaves and blossoms.
3. Hook the tiny pods where the edges are completely visible with light values.
4. Hook the pods that are covered up with medium values.
5. Fill in all the empty spaces with dark values.

There are two other ways to approach this flower: proddy all the blossoms or pixelate a small lupine that is included in a pictorial cottage garden. ✺

CHAPTER THIRTEEN

Flower Shapes—Trumpets, Tubes, Funnels, and Cones

"Just living is not enough," said the butterfly. "One must have sunshine, freedom and a little flower."
—Hans Christian Andersen

The flowers in this section are cone shaped. The stamens catch the light, pulling the eye into the bottom of the cone. A lily is a trumpet with its stamens protruding outward. Other flowers, such as the calla lily, start conical and then flare out into a trumpet shape. Some plants are combinations of tubes and bells, like foxgloves and angel trumpets. All of their petals curve into a center point.

Angel Trumpet (*Brugmansia*)

This strikingly beautiful subtropical flower is a member of the potato family. The plant is a shower of multiple blossoms, and its elongated leaves hang like brightly colored trumpets on the vine.

Colors: White, peach, pink, and yellow. Blue trumpets with dark navy blue anthers are an unusual variety. Yellow, pink, and peach combinations are the most familiar. The turned-up tips often are a different color than the petals.

Petals: The petals look like hanging trumpets turning upward into pointed tips. Petal veins follow the length of the trumpet, but you have to look closely to see them. Underneath the wings are dark shadows. The blossom's dimensions are approximately 10" long by 4" wide.

Flower center: The green and yellow center is often hidden from view.

Leaves and stems: The triangular leaves and flowers are connected to the branches by the yellow-green receptacle. The leaves, including the receptacle, are as long as the entire flower. Their edges are either wavy or smooth.

Rating: 7

Challenge: The challenge in hooking *Angels Among Us* was to select the best shade of pink for the petals. A

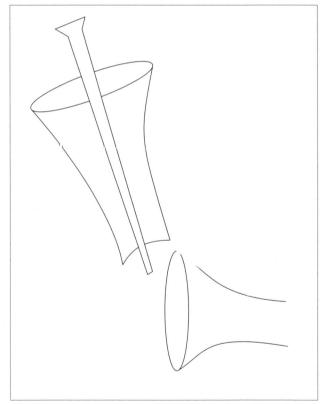

Geometric Representation of Trumpet, Tube, Funnel, and Cone-Shaped Flowers,
ink on Canson paper.

pale pink blossom that could be intensified against a dark background was the aim. A new Pro Chemical dye called Peach Blossom was too flat. The dye formulas listed on page 106 turned out to work perfectly.

Materials: Dip dyes

Angels Among Us, *28" x 34", #8-cut and hand-ripped strip wool on linen. Designed and hooked by Jane Halliwell Green, Edgewater, Maryland, 2011.*

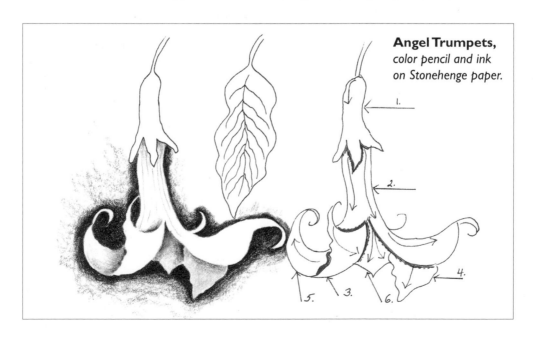

Angel Trumpets, *color pencil and ink on Stonehenge paper.*

1.
2.
5. 3. 6. 4.

Dyeing *For Angels Among Us*

Angels Dip Dye Petals: The dip dyed strips for the petals are 36" long and 12" wide. Three pinks were dyed for the long petals. Be sure to overlap the three formulas.

> ❧ Primary Fusion #11 (*page 49*) was dipped first.

> ❧ $1/64$ tsp. Red-Violet (MC) dissolved in 1 c. hot water was placed in a second pan. The center of my strip was dipped in this dye.

> ❧ The last color was $1/32$ Aqualon Pink (C) dissolved in 1 c. of hot water. This is the light part of the dip.

Shadows: Shadows and petal tips were leftovers from a previous project.

Bold yellow-green: PF #34.

> $1/4$ tsp. Yellow #119 (PC)
> $1/64$ tsp. Blue #490 (PC)
> $1/64$ tsp. Black #672 (PC)

Dissolve all three dyes in 1 c. of hot water. From this dye make a gradation.

Background: Antique black

How to Hook

The large 36" x 36" wall hanging was hooked with a #8 cut and 1" ripped strips. The veins were hooked with a #4 cut. It is important to include the detail of the veins because excluding them will result in a big pink blob.

Angel trumpets and their leaves appear to hang downward; therefore, they should also be hooked in that direction.

1. Start with the stem and receptacle. Use a bright yellow-green.
2. Hook the petal veins in a narrow cut. They extend almost to the outer edge. Space them about ½" apart. Make sure they curve. It may be necessary to try a variety of materials. Start by selecting a fabric that is one or two values darker than the petal.
3. Hook the area between veins with the dip-dyed fabric. Lay the loops up against the veins that have already established the flow and curve of the petal.
4. For the shadows that fall underneath the turned-up and overlapped petals, use a dark value.
5. The leaves were hooked with a variety of light greens. The leaf veins are the same dark pink used to shadow the flowers.
6. The background is antique black and complements the lighter flowers wonderfully.

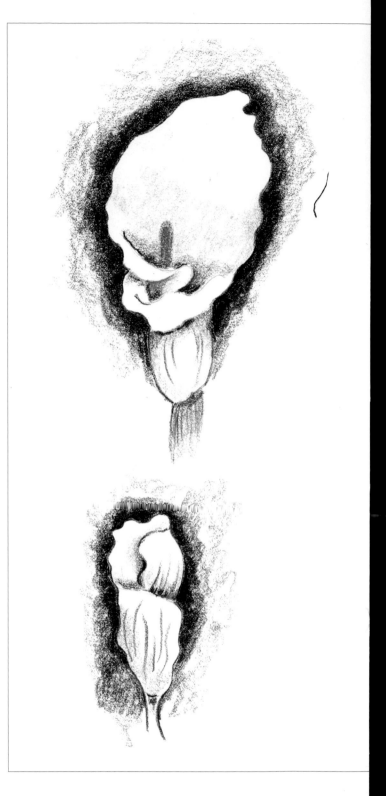

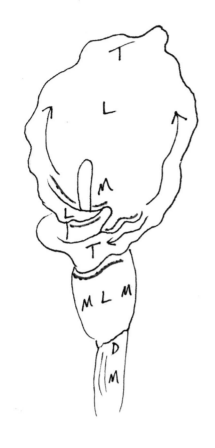

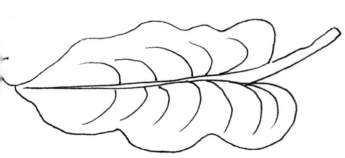

Calla Lily, *color pencil and ink on Stonehenge paper.*

number of other colors including yellow, orange, pink, green, dark purple, bronze-red, and peach.

Petals: The flower is known for its dramatic smooth petals set in a rolled shape and subtle veining.

Flower center: A single yellow-orange spike.

Leaves and stems: The leaves are large and triangular with white or silver colored speckles. They emerge off of a thick and tall stem. The veins have beautiful curves as they come off the mid-rib.

Rating: 4

Challenges: Finding the correct value for the shadows around the spike and under the curve of the lip is one challenge. Another is depicting the smooth and elegant appearance of this plant using woolen fabric. Because loops are less apparent with a smaller cut, use a #3 cut and the surface of the petal will appear smoother.

Materials: Dip dyes plus additional shadow color

How to Hook

The calla lily has distinct veins. On a white calla lily, they are yellow-green. Hook a few of these, but limit the quantity.

1. Start with the center spike. In a wall hanging, sculpt the center.
2. Hook the lightest petal roll horizontally, following the curve of the roll.
3. Starting at the base of the petal either to the right or left of the spike, hook from dark to light. Be sure to curve the lines.

Calla Lily White

For a white calla lily, tint white wool with a little color. Try purple, blue, green, or a pink tint placed at the bottom of the dip. Cover 10% to 20% of the strip with color leaving the remainder white. If the white seems harsh, soften it with a wash of Maize (C), Ecru (C), or Old Ivory (C).

Calla Lily (*Zantedeschia*)

This elegant tropical flower from South Africa resembles a trumpet shaped out of rolled paper. Its name comes from the Greek word for beautiful. The dramatic flower grows on stalks 2' high. It is a popular wedding flower, and it is not a lily.

Colors: Calla lilies are known for their pale green or white hues, but they are also available in an incredible

Daffodil (*Narcissus*)

> *"I wandered lonely as a cloud*
> *That floats on high o'er vales and hills,*
> *When all at once I saw a crowd,*
> *A host of golden daffodils . . ."*
> —William Wordsworth

Daffodils are one of the most popular flowers in the world. The spring flower is native to Europe, North Africa, and Asia and is often referred to as a jonquil. The flowers symbolize friendship and prosperity. Daffodils have a corona in the center that looks like a trumpet surrounded by a ring of petals. There are many species, and new ones are created each year.

Colors: We associate yellow with daffodils; however orange, white, pink, peach, and numerous other combinations are possible. The trumpet may be a different color than the ring of petals. Bulb catalogs are a wonderful reference for all the color possibilities.

Petals: The daffodil always has six petals. The cylindrical part of the flower may be surrounded with ruffles that hide the trumpet, or the trumpet may protrude from a circle of ruffles.

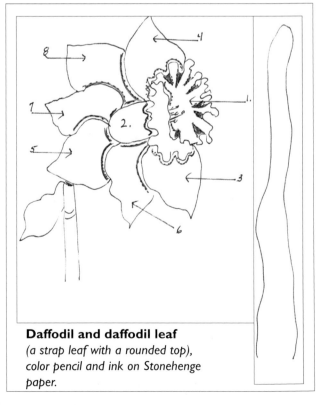

Daffodil and daffodil leaf
(a strap leaf with a rounded top),
color pencil and ink on Stonehenge
paper.

Spring Reflections, *27" x 43", #5-cut wool on linen. Designed by Jane Halliwell Green and hooked by Lynne Fowler, Onancock, Virginia, 2010.*

Amelia's Daffodil,
*24" x 24", #2- to 5-cut
wool on linen. Adapted
from a watercolor
by Janice Sumler and
hooked by Marian Hall,
Chester, Pennsylvania,
2008.* MARIAN HALL

Flower center: Daffodils have green stamens and yellow anthers.

Leaves and stems: The stem is usually bent at the top due to the weight of the large flower. There is a thin and wrinkled gold flap attached to the stem, which was the original casing for the bud. The flowers are surrounded by long linear strap leaves that are slightly curved at the top.

Rating: 6

Challenges: The shadows are challenging in this flower, particularly if you choose a yellow daffodil and if there are many ruffles around the circle. Remember that these ruffles fall where the edge of the flower dips inward.

Materials: 6- to 8-value swatch

Shadows: Acceptable shadow colors for a yellow daffodil are orange, yellow-orange, yellow-green, or violet. Yellow and violet are complementary colors, making violet the best choice. The challenge lies in choosing the correct value. If the shade is too light it will disappear. If it is too dark it will look like an outline. When Marian Hall hooked *Amelia's Daffodil*, she managed the shadows using a variety of green-gold colors. The forward-facing petal was outlined with purple to make it stand out.

How to Hook

1. Start with the center and underline the circular area with a dark shadow.

2. Hook the stamens and anthers. Depending on the size of the flower, one tail or two loops may be sufficient. Squeeze dark shadows between them.

3. If the flower is large enough, realistic ruffles can be hooked from the outside in toward the stamens. The ruffles are placed where the edge of the flower bends inward creating the shadow. A simpler approach is to hook around the outside circle with the lightest value working toward the stamens.

4. Proceed to the central trumpet. Place a shadow line under the lip of the ruffles. Hook this horizontally. Medium values are on the outer edges of the trumpet and the lightest value is in the center.

5. Hook Petal 1 first from dark to light. In a 6-value swatch, a medium-light value may be deep enough to shadow the base of the petal against the trumpet. If not, try medium or dark shades. It may be necessary to skip values in areas where shadow lines are indicated.

6. Continue with Petals 2 through 6, getting progressively darker.

7. The separation between the sections of the flowers should be clear.

   In Lynne Fowler's contemporary rug, *Spring Reflections (page 109)*, the background is hooked with a variety of dark purples. Lynne carries the yellow color around the design by capturing it in the bubbles.

Foxglove (*Digitalis*)

The tall foxglove plant is a collection of simple cone-shaped blossoms growing on a single cylindrical stem. It is a woodland plant. The stem can be as tall as 5' with the 1" blossoms so small they can fit over a fingertip.

Colors: Purple, light gray, white, pink, and red-violet

Petals: The blossom looks like an elongated upside-down bell. At the base of the petal there are lots of small sepals.

Flower center: This part of the flower is sometimes referred to as the mouth. The dark maroon spots, which are generally on a cream background, are the distinguishing characteristic of the plant. The spots must be included. Omitting them would be like forgetting to put your shoes on in the morning! Use a very dark red, such as burgundy or maroon.

Leaves and stems: The leaves are oblong, smooth and heavily veined. The flower stems wrap around the wide stalk.

Rating: 2

Challenge: The greatest challenge is seeing the difference between the tube and the mouth. If the values are too close then these two areas will merge together and the flower will look like a blob.

Materials: A foxglove can be hooked with a 4-value swatch.

How to Hook

An entire stalk of flowers should taper from a narrow top to a wider bottom. The buds at the top are small, but as the flowers emerge on the lower stalk the tall triangular appearance is unmistakable.

To dye wool for this flower, use Primary Fusion #10 (*page 44*), Primary Fusion #11 (*page 49*), and White Magic (*page 46*).

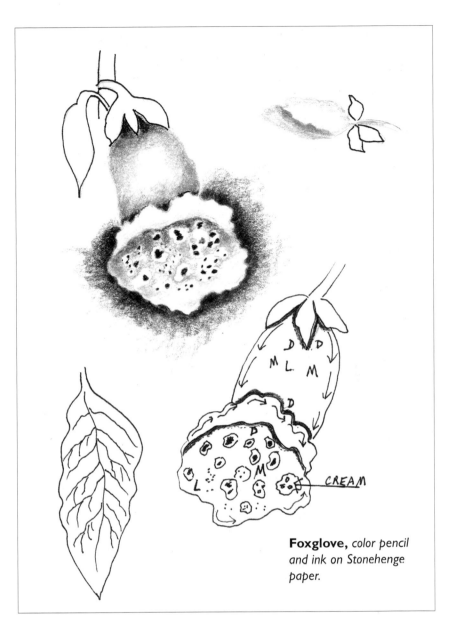

Foxglove, *color pencil and ink on Stonehenge paper.*

1. Start by hooking the top buds and flowers first and work down the stalk. Closed buds sit at the peak. As you move down the stalk, the tightly closed buds begin to open until the full flower makes its appearance. There are numerous flowers stacked on top of each other. The upper blossoms are light while the lower ones are darker, because shadows are cast upon them by the blossoms above.
2. Hook the light upper lip first.
3. Hook the sepals at the base of the flower.
4. Hook the tube. The middle is light, and the area under the lip is heavily shadowed.
5. Finally, hook the mouth. Hook the dark markings in a variety of shapes. Surround them with medium values near the lip and lighter ones at the edge.
6. The difference between the tube and the mouth should be clearly evident.

Hibiscus (*Hibiscus*)

Hibiscus means delicate beauty. While a student in Florida, I was surrounded by plate-sized hibiscus blossoms in every color one could imagine. I fell in love with this tropical flower and have hooked and painted it at least fifty times! There are no less than 220 species.

Colors: Bright red, yellow, pink, salmon, gold, white, and lavender. The stamen must have a different color or value than the petals. Choose from green, yellow, orange, and white.

Petals: Five large, flat, and magnificent trumpet-shaped petals have distinct veins. These are the hardest part of the flower to hook.

Flower center: A long stamen surges out of a curved area that I call the smile. If the hibiscus lacks the smile, the flower may lose its characteristic appearance. In the hibiscus illustration, the smile is directly under the base of the stamen (A). The anthers at the top of the stamen are fuzzy. The dark area at the base of the stamen fans out into the three upper petals. The stamens are dramatic. They can fall far outside the petal or, depending on the variety, be considerably shorter.

Leaves and stems: The leaves are wide, oval, and ragged.

Rating: 4

Challenges: Choosing the right value for the veins and hooking the stamen in a color that stands out against the petal are two challenges.

Materials: Dip dyes are the first choice for a hibiscus. In addition to the dipped strips, dye a very dark color in order to have enough value changes between the petals to the left and to the right side of the stamen. A 6- to 8-value swatch is another choice.

How to Hook

Primary Fusion #42 (*page 95*) makes a beautiful yellow-orange dye for a hibiscus. Primary Fusion #11 (*page 49*) is also a wonderful dark base for the petals of both pink and yellow flowers. Other good color choices are a red-violet base in a white petal; a red-violet base in a pink petal; a red-violet base to an orange petal; deep brown red to a red petal; and red-violet base in a yellow petal.

1. Start with the stamen. Choose a color or value that will be different than the petal. If you use the same color as the petal, it must be lighter or darker. In

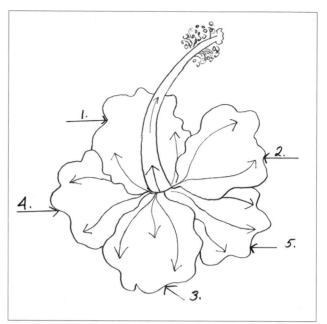

Hibiscus, *ink on Stonehenge paper.*

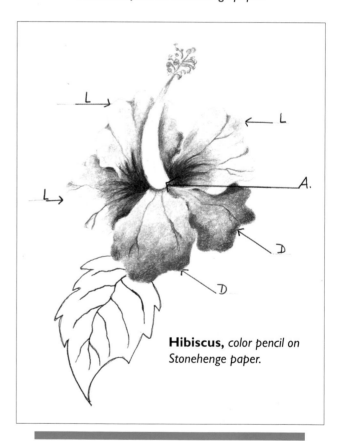

Hibiscus, *color pencil on Stonehenge paper.*

Pink Reef
⅛ tsp. Wild Rose (C)
⅛ tsp. Cherry (C)
Dissolve both dyes in 1 c. of hot water.
Dip most of the strip in the pink,
and tip it off with ¹⁄₃₂ tsp.
#119 Yellow (PC) dissolved in 1 c. of hot water.
Use the same yellow for the stamen.

A single hibiscus in **Botanical Fantasy.** *See full rug on page 23.*

Botanical Fantasy, the stamen on the right is a lighter value than the petal and the stamen on the left is a light yellow. This yellow is the same used for the highlights at the edge of the petals. If the stamen is light and protrudes into a light background, you must change value at the petal's edge.

2. Pixelate the anthers at the tips of the stamen. A loop and two tails, or two loops and two tails are needed.

3. Hook the veins. The veins should be darker than the petal color. If they are too dark they will stick out. The veins and the stamen colors often come out of the scrap bag. Be prepared for reverse hooking (pulling out a strip) until you feel you have it right. Put the petal color in first before you start reverse hooking, as you can't evaluate the effect until you see quite a bit of the petal hooked.

4. Hook the dark area at the base of the top three petals. This method is reminiscent of how we hooked a pansy's whiskers. Leave a bit of space between the spikes to insert some of the petal color. Place a small amount (about one row) beneath the smile.

5. Hook the lightest petal (#1) from the dark base to the light tip.

6. Continue with the remaining four petals. The two lower petals are hooked from light (beneath the smile) to a darker outer edge. Make sure you adjust the values between the petals so that the separate petals can be clearly identified.

7. Make final adjustments to the veins.

8. Hook the stamen in a contrasting color.

Day Lilies Close Up, *81" x 34", hand-ripped 1" strips of wool on linen.*
Designed and hooked by Jane Halliwell Green, Edgewater, Maryland, 2011.

Lily (*Lilium*)

"I am my beloved's, and my beloved is mine; he feedeth among the lilies."—Solomon 2:1–2

Lilies could be the most popular flower in the world. They have been artistic, literary, and Christian symbols for centuries. The white lily symbolizes modesty and virginity; the orange lily, passion; the Easter lily, the Virgin Mary. The daylily got its name because each blossom only lasts one day. Lilies come in different shapes, sizes, and colors. There are 100 known species occurring in all parts of the northern hemisphere. It is believed that lilies have been cultivated longer than any other flower, dating back to the eighteenth dynasty of Egypt. Two of the popular lilies in rug hooking are the star gazer and the tiger lily.

Colors: Star gazer lilies are white, yellow, cream, orange and pink, red, and salmon pink. Tiger lilies are orange, red, burnt orange, and salmon red.

Petals: Lilies have six petals. In some lilies you will see a scattering of freckles toward the base of the petals.

Bud: The bud looks like a fat hot dog. There are veins on both sides. The buds are yellow-green or yellow with a hint of the blossom's color.

Flower centers: The stamens are yellow-green. The anthers are rust to maroon and are an oblong shape. The pistil is yellow, rust, or yellow-green. The star-shaped center on a star gazer lily is a common characteristic. This can be seen in *Seeing Stars*, the pattern included in this book.

Leaves and stems: There are smooth narrow leaves coming off of a tall stalk. The distinctive veining runs the length of the leaf as shown in the illustration.

Rating: 3

Challenge: The many turnovers make parts of this flower difficult.

Materials: Dip dyes with an extra piece of dark for the shadows and freckles

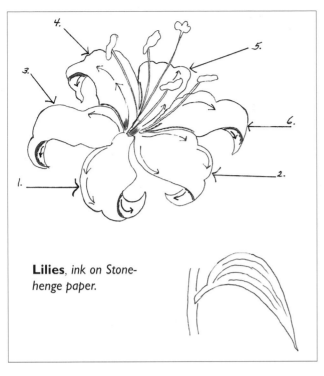

Lilies, *ink on Stonehenge paper.*

How to Hook

1. Hook the stamens, pistil, and anthers before hooking the petals.
2. The center of the flower is darker unless you are portraying a lily with a yellow center, or the daylily, which has a star.
3. Start with the top and lightest petal. In a daylily petals often turn inward. When this happens there may be a lighter area in the center of the petal. Also be aware that one or more of the six petals can create a shadow on the petal next to it.
4. In this lily, the three upper petals are dark to light, but the three lower ones are light to dark. The turnovers are hooked dark to light. The anthers are dark rust, and the pistils are light.
5. Don't forget the freckles! Hook them with two tails and no loops.

Lilies, *color pencil on Stonehenge paper.*

The rug *Day Lilies* is a close up hooked with 1"-wide ripped strips. I was inspired by a photograph in a seed catalog. I cropped the picture and hooked the three lilies in the center. I used the leaves and stems to create an abstract connection between the flowers, and then filled them in with a dark blue-green. It was hooked in just less than three weeks. My dip dyes were approximately 36" to 52" long.

Morning Glory (*Ipomoea*)

The morning glory was discovered in China and its seeds were used for medicinal purposes. The Japanese, however, cultivated it as an ornamental plant beginning in the ninth century. Because this is a climbing plant, the twists and turns of the stems create interesting design possibilities. Use this flower to embellish fences, arbors, and gates.

Colors: Blue, lavender, pink, white, and red

Petals: Morning glories only have one blossom but its single petal is divided into units by veins. The ruffles and shadows occur at the edge of the petal where the veins emerge. Notice a slight dip at the edge of the petal in every place where there is a vein.

Flower centers: A small touch of yellow in the pistil is surrounded by a light color: white, cream, or a pale pink.

Buds: The twisting motion of the bud can be achieved by watching your values. Each section is hooked dark to light and then back to dark once more. There are sepals and long twisting tendrils at the base of the bud.

Leaves and stems: The heart-shaped leaves are smooth and come to a sharp point at the end. The stems twine around all kinds of supports.

Rating: 5. The larger the flower, the easier it is to hook.

Challenge: Hooking a gentle curve from the center of the flower out to the edge is difficult. The lines often end up too straight.

Materials: Dip dyes are recommended for large morning glories, but the smaller ones are easier to handle with a 6-value swatch.

How to Hook

The illustrations show two different ways of hooking this flower. Working from the interior toward the edge and fingering the values is shown in (A). Hooking around the outer edge and into the center is an easier approach for new rug hookers (B).

1. Start with the yellow dot in the center. In a small flower the center is a loop with two tails.
2. Divide the flower into sections using the veins as the outer edges. Start by hooking the vein, which is slightly darker than the flower color. Note that the ruffle or shadow usually occurs where the vein dips

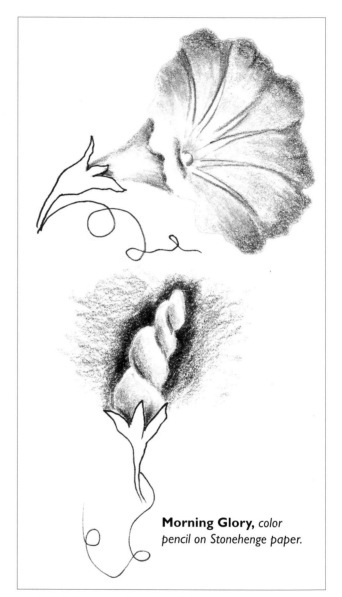

Morning Glory, *color pencil on Stonehenge paper.*

slightly lower at the edge of the petal.

3. If you are fingering the flower realistically, start near the center with your light material and gently finger values out to the edge. Note that the curve is very important. Hug the vein and you will have no problem keeping this curve.
4. If you are hooking around the petal, make the edge your darkest value. When you end at the vein, clip. Do not carry your wool under the vein.
5. Follow the shaded illustration showing how the bud twists and how the values range from dark to light to dark again. There must be enough contrast between the light top and the dark base to make the bud twist.

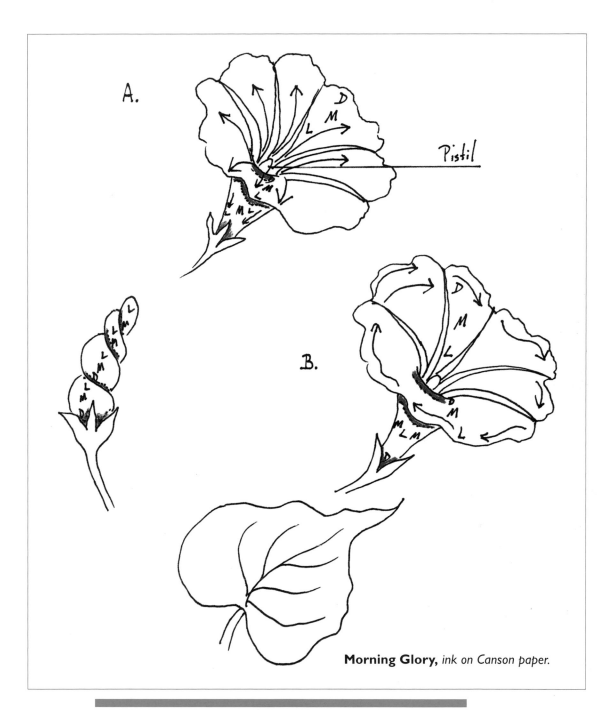

Morning Glory, *ink on Canson paper.*

PR110

This is a formula in Prisms 2. It can be used as a swatch or a dip dye.
It is a half strength version of the original formula.
Dissolve all four dyes in 1 c. of hot water.
⅛ tsp. Blue #425C (PC)
⅛ tsp. Blue #490 (PC)
1/16 tsp. Navy #413 (PC)
1/16 tsp. Black #672 (PC)

A good color combination is a pale pink center
in combination with PR110. Aqualon pink (C) is a pale pink. Start
with 1/32 tsp. dissolved in 1 c.
1/64 tsp. will give you barely a tint of pink.
Dip a small part of the strip in the pink followed by the blue.

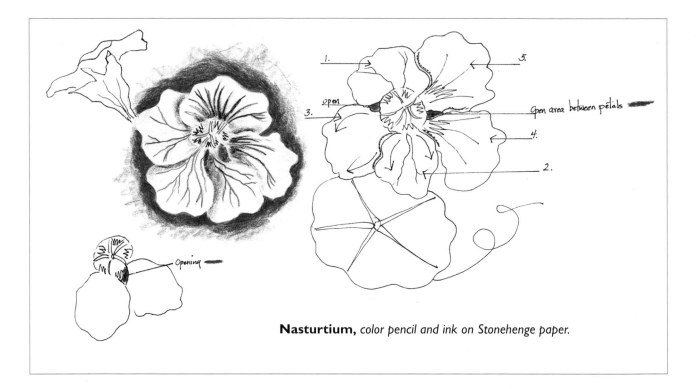

Nasturtium, *color pencil and ink on Stonehenge paper.*

Nasturtium (*Tropaeolum*)

This funnel-shaped flower, native to South America, is an edible flower. Do not be surprised to see it pop up in salads and sandwiches at your local restaurant. It grows easily as a bush, climber, or trailer. You'll see it hugging the ground in most rock gardens, where it spreads rapidly.

Colors: Yellow, gold, pink, white, orange, peach, and combinations of all

Petals: The five petals are heavily veined. At the base of the upper two petals are dark patches with darker veins emerging from them. On a yellow or peach nasturtium, the patch and veins might be a dark maroon. Behind the cutouts is the funnel-shaped tube.

Flower center: The center of a nasturtium is delicate and lacy. The stamens and filaments are yellow. Behind these delicate parts is the yellow-green funnel that makes the entire center look like one color. Along the base of the petal, teethlike projections surround the center.

Note the shape of the interior of the flower. Study the nasturtium drawing. Getting the correct shape in the center will identify the blossom as a nasturtium. The open spaces between the flower center and the petals are distinguishing characteristics and are important elements to capture.

Leaves and stems: The leaves are round with yellow veins. The primary veins radiate out from a distinct spot in the center of the leaf. They form a star. Smaller extensions flow out from these primary veins in a delicate lace pattern. The edges of these distinctive leaves are slightly yellow, as though someone drew a thin line of yellow magic marker around the edge.

Rating: 8

Challenge: Capturing the delicate, lacelike quality of the flower's center and the many spiderlike veins.

Materials: Swatch and dip dyes. Shadow colors can be a dark value of the petal color or complement.

How to Hook

1. Start with the center. If you get this part right, the entire flower will "read" as a nasturtium. Hook the starlike filaments and the toothlike projections with yellow. Fill around them with a strong and medium value of yellow-green.

2. Continue on to the two back petals. These are the ones with the dark patches near the center. The dark patches emerge with the same color into the spider-like veins. Unlike some flowers, the veins in a nasturtium can be many values darker than the petal. Because of this, it will take trial and error to get the right combination of petal and vein. The veins should be subtle, so hook them in a narrow cut.

3. Finish the remaining petals. The three front petals do not have the dark patches, but they do have the veins.

4. Hook the leaves with yellow veins. Round leaves have lots of speckles, so look for a spot dye. A solid color with a heavy amount of dark abrash will also do.

Petunia (*Petunia*)

Petunias originated in Argentina. They are available in a wide variety of shapes, sizes, and colors and are single, double, ruffled, smooth, or frilly-edged blooms. Petals come striped, veined, or in solid colors. The ruffled petunia is the more popular variety and is composed of one cone-shaped petal with five scallops around the top. The scallops look like five distinct petals, but they separate about one-third of the way down.

Petunias offer us a great opportunity to jazz up our rugs because they are so flamboyant. Moreover, there are so many color choices that it makes color planning easy.

Colors: The petunia comes in an incredible range of colors. Almost anything is possible! There are white, pink, purple, magenta, mauve, and yellow-speckled, striped, or veined varieties. Look for big contrasts such as white and scarlet red, or indigo blue and pale yellow.

Petals: The single petal has five scallops. The petals have obvious veins. Hook the veins slightly darker than the petal or in a contrasting color. The edges of the petals can be wavy or ruffled.

Flower center: The pistil is yellow-green.

Leaves and stems: The leaves are hairy, oval, and very small.

Rating: 6

Challenge: The distinct veins, turnovers, and many ruffles all combine to present some serious challenges.

Materials: Swatches

Petunias, *color pencil and ink on Stonehenge paper.*

How to Hook

1. Tackle this flower by dividing it up into manageable sections between the dominant veins.
2. Hook the yellow center.
3. Hook the veins from the center outward. Some petunias have light veins and other varieties have dark ones.
4. Hook each section between the veins.
5. The trumpet is often a yellow-green with distinct veins. ✺

CHAPTER FOURTEEN

Seeing Stars

> *"In his garden every man may be his own artist/ Without apology or explanation."* —Louise Beebe Wilder

A Hooked Wall Hanging

Seeing Stars was inspired by a watercolor of the same name. The distinctive star shape in the center of the star gazer lily is repeated in the background. The hooked version has a quality never possible in a painting: it sparkles! Adding yarn embedded with metallic sequins makes the sparkle possible.

This small 16" x 20" wall hanging hooked with a #4 cut on cotton warp cloth can be resized to any dimension you choose. A local copy center will resize it for you, or you can modify it with a computer program.

The challenge in hooking the flowers is the overlap between the two lilies. The value between the petals must be dark enough for the flowers to be seen clearly.

Use dip dyes to hook the flowers. I cut the wool into 16" and 18" strips and found an intense and bright pink in Primary Fusion #10 (*page 44*). Dyeing additional dark strips of PF #10 for the shadows was not dark enough—or different enough—to shape the flowers and separate the two lilies from each other. So I dipped the darkest pink strips again in a dye bath of purple. This violet shadow turned out to be perfect between most of the petals.

Seeing Stars, *ink on Strathmore paper.*

Seeing Stars, *18" x 20", #4-cut wool on cotton warp cloth.*
Designed and hooked by Jane Halliwell Green, Edgewater, Maryland, 2011.

How to Hook the Flowers

Use Primary Fusion #34 to dye colors for the flower center and Primary Fusion # 10 (*page 44*) for the flowers. The shadows between the flower petals were pink strips over dyed with ¼ tsp. Violet #818 (PC) dissolved in 1 c. hot water.

1. Hook the center of the upper lily. The star in the center is outlined with one row of Mandarin Gold and filled with a yellow-green (Primary Fusion #34). Hook the stamens and anthers. Use the same yellow-green for the stamens and a piece of dark red scrap wool for the anthers.

2. There is no star in the bottom lily, so hook the stamens and anthers exactly like the upper flower. The lower lily is the largest flower, so those petals will be tackled first. Hook the lightest petals first. The shadow areas are indicated with dotted red lines. Work from the base of the petal to the tip. Add the freckles on the petals by tucking in a few single loops that are cut.

3. Proceed to the upper lily and do the same.

4. Note that there are two Xs in the area between the lilies to indicate an area of background material.

How to Hook the Stars

Hook the two stars with Mandarin Gold. Leave a small area in the center of the stars open. These open areas will be hooked later with yellow bridal netting covered with gold flecks. Cut the netting fabric at least 1" wide and pull the loops higher than all the rest. The bright fabric will draw attention to the lilies. Do not worry if the loops are not even. Fill the two stars farther away from the flowers with a light blue-green wool.

How to Hook the Tendrils

The tendrils were hooked with CM 40 Painted Desert from Prisms #3 *Color in Motion.* This spot-dyed fabric was perfect as all the colors in the rug appear.

How to Hook the Leaves

Hook the veins with dark pink strips left over from the flowers. A piece of light yellow-green wool from the scrap bag filled in the leaves.

How to Hook the Background

The background really makes this piece. This background is exactly like the noodle background described in Chapter 4, but the materials were dyed specifically for this piece.

Follow this rule for a background like this: mix materials sitting side-by-side and shoulder-to-shoulder on the color clock that are of the same value. This will result in a background with movement and subtle changes of color.

I chose a dark background in the following colors: green, blue-green, and blue. I cut lots of strips from each fabric and mixed them together so they would enter the rug randomly. One plaid was a true green with a dark purple and red-violet stripe. The plaid added the slightest bit of pink and purple. In addition, a wool, silk, and bamboo blend yarn with metallic sequins, called Yang and imported from China, added the sparkle. It was not the easiest yarn to hook, but it was well worth the effort. Yang helped to make the name, *Seeing Stars*, the right title for this piece!

How to Hook the Border

I finished *Seeing Stars* by hooking one row of the spot dye Fireworks (*page 45*) around the outside. This fabric carried the dominant pinks and purples to the edge and balanced the colors. Use Fireworks to dye colors for the border. ☙

Mandarin Gold—Stars
From the book Prisms #1, dye
the color for the stars over ½ yard
of white or natural wool.
⅛ tsp. Yellow #199C (PC)
1/64 tsp. Chestnut #560 (PC)
Dissolve both dyes in 1 c. of hot water.
Pour half the formula in the pan, and use
the other half to pour directly on top
of the material as an abrash.

Painted Desert—Tendrils
Dye this color over ½ yard of natural wool
and handle it as a spot dye
(from the book Prisms #3).
⅛ tsp. Yellow #119 (PC) dissolved in 1 c. water
1/32 tsp. Red #349 (PC) dissolved in 1 c. hot water
1/128 tsp. Turquoise #478 (PC)
dissolved in 1 c. hot water

CHAPTER FIFTEEN

Floral Gallery

Sunflowers, *28" x 53", #6-, 7-, and 8-cut wool on linen. Designed by Charco patterns and hooked by Linda Gustafson, Chardon, Ohio, 2009.* RICK PORTER

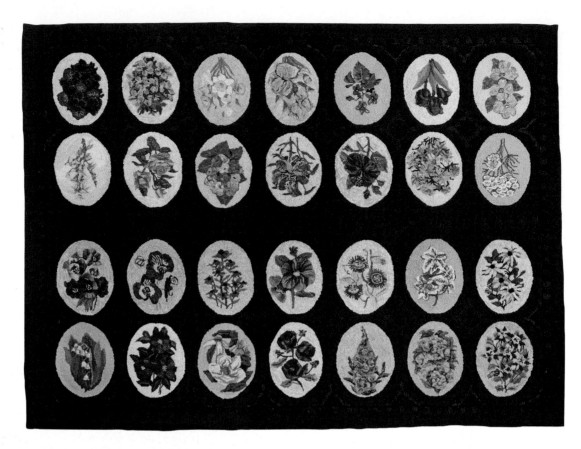

Mother's Garden, *49" x 64", #4- and 5-cut wool on linen. Designed by Phil and Sarah Province and hooked by Sarah Province, Silver Spring, Maryland, 2009.*

Sarah's husband, Phil, laid out the design for Sarah. She had twenty-eight ovals and had to select her favorite flowers to fill them. Sarah says, "My fingers flew in hooking this rug. Each one was like a little rug by itself." She varied the soft pastel backgrounds of each flower.

Prodded Parakeet, *14" square, #8-cut and hand-cut wool on linen. Designed and hooked by Gene Shepherd, Anaheim, California, 2009.* GENE SHEPHERD

Little Buckingham, *24" x 36", #3-cut wool on cotton. Designed by Jane McGown Flynn and hooked by Lissa Williamson, Severna Park, Maryland, 2010.* LISSA WILLIAMSON

Rose and Lattice, *21" x 26", #4-cut wool on cotton warp. Designed by Fraser Rugs and hooked by Toni Breeding, Queen Anne, Maryland, 2010.*

Provincial and Territorial Flowers of Canada, *30½" x 60", #3- and 4-cut wool on linen.*
Designed and hooked by Abbie Ross, Springhill, Nova Scotia, Canada, 2008. ABBIE ROSS
This outstanding rug celebrates the flowers of Canada. Starting at the bottom left, going clockwise, and ending at the
Canadian Flag are a white trillium, prairie crocus, western red lily, wild rose, Pacific dogwood, fireweed, mountain avens, purple
saxifraga, pitcher plant, lady's slipper, mayflower, purple violet, and a blue flag iris.

Long Flower Basket,
24" x 54", #8-cut wool on linen. Adapted from M. Shaw painting, Spruce Ridge Studio, and hooked by Pat Seliga, St. Louis, Missouri, 2005.
PAT SELIGA

African Violets, *16" x 19", wool on cotton warp cloth. Designed and hooked by Jane Halliwell Green, Edgewater, Maryland, 2009. Each blossom has a tiny blue bead sewn into the center.*

Gray's Circle, *46" x 51", #3-cut wool on cotton rug warp. Designed by Pearl McGown and hooked by Lynne Fowler, Onancock, Virginia, 2008.*

Basket of Flowers, *18" x 24", more than 50 unusual materials including flannel and wool in all cuts and many types of yarn on monk's cloth. Designed and hooked by Sally D'Albora, Rockville, Maryland, 2010.*

Rapture Plus Four, *14" x 56", #3-cut wool on cotton. Designed by Jane McGown Flynn and hooked by Jane Halliwell Green, Edgewater, Maryland, 1998.*

Roses, *39" x 39", #3-cut wool on burlap. Designed by Pearl McGown and hooked by Betty Kerr, Chestertown, Maryland, 1998.*

Baby in the Rose,
24" x 36", #3- and 4-cut wool on linen. Designed and hooked by Ruth Mills Smith, Springhill, Nova Scotia, Canada, 2004.

The child in the center of Ruth's beautiful rose rug is her granddaughter, Zoe. Zoe was the last of eight grandchildren born in Ruth's family. She was a very ill baby and Ruth decided to hook this rug for her. Zoe recovered and is the proud seven-year-old owner of this beautiful hooked rug.

Oxford Gardens, *20" x 24", wool, yarn, and unspun wool on linen. Designed and hooked by Jane Halliwell Green, Edgewater, Maryland, 2009.*

Funky Flowers, *36" x 36", #8-cut wool on linen. Designed by Kathy Meentemeyer (Dream Catcher Designs) and hooked by Pat Seliga, St. Louis, Missouri, 2009. The dip dyes are 36" x 36".*

Prodded Wreath, *14" square, #10-cut and hand-torn shaped wool on linen. Designed and hooked by Gene Shepherd, Anaheim, California, 2011.*
GENE SHEPHERD

Sultan's Palace, *36½" x 61", #3-cut wool on cotton warp cloth. Designed by Jeanne Benjamin (New Earth Designs) and hooked by Ginny Fan, Ellicott City, Maryland, 2007.*

- *Jane Halliwell Green*
  PO Box 842
  Edgewater, MD 21037
  410–200–1143
  jane@janehalliwell.com
  www.rugandwool.com
  Color Clock Workbook is available at
  www.rugandwool.com

- *Prisms #1, #2, and #3 Dye Books*
  44 Stearns Ave.
  Johnson City, NY 13790
  Clair De Roos: c_deroos@juno.com
  Nancy MacLennan: nancymac18@
  juno.com

- *Primary Fusion: A Guide to Dyeing
  With Only Three Primary Colors*
  Multiple Fusion Spots
  Ingrid Hieronimus
  RR#2, Petersburg, Ontario
  NOB 2HO
  519–578–0826
  raggtyme@rughookinghome.com
  www.rughookinghome.com

- *For additional information about
  prodded flowers: Gene Shepherd*
  gene@geneshepherd.com
  www.Geneshepherd.com

- *Dorr Mill Store*
  PO Box 88
  Hale Street
  Guild, NH 03754
  (Supplies)
  800–846–3677
  www.dorrmillstore.com

- *Harry M. Fraser Company*
  PO Box 939
  Stoneville. NC 27048
  336–573–9830
  (Supplies)
  fraserrugs@aol.com

- *W. Cushing and Company*
  21 North Street
  Kennebunkport, ME 04046
  1–800–626–7847
  (Source for Cushing Dyes)
  www.wcushing.com

- *PRO Chemical and Dye Company*
  PO Box 14
  Somerset, MA 02726
  (Source for Pro Chem dyes)

- *Rittermere-Hurst-Field*
  PO Box 487
  Aurora, Ontario, Canada
  L4G 3L6
  (Source for Majic Carpet Dyes)
  800–268–9813
  www.LetsHookRugs.com

- *Seaside Rug Hooking*
  www.SeasideRugHookingCompany.com
  (Source for Jacqueline Hansen
  designs)

- *House of Price*
  rughook@earthlink.net
  1–877–784–4665
  (Source of Charco and McGown
  patterns)

- *Rapid Resizer*
  A computer program to enlarge
  designs.
  www.rapidresizer.com

- *Rug Hookers Network*
  www.rughookersnetwork.com to locate a
  teacher

Bulb Catalogs and Publications Featuring Flowers

- *Schreiners Iris Lover's Catalog*
  3625 Quinaby Road, N.E. Dept 36
  Salem, OR 97303
  www.schreinersgardens.com
  1–800–525–2367

- *John Scheepers Inc.*
  23 Tulip Dr
  Bantam, CT 06750
  860–567–0838
  www.johnscheepers.com

- *Burpee Seeds*
  W. Atlee Burpee & Co.
  Order a catalog at *www.burpee.com*

- *Birds and Bloom*
  1–800–344–6913
  Rpsubcustomercare@custhelp.com
  PO Box 5294
  Harlan, Iowa 51593

- *Brecks Dutch Bulbs*
  www.dutchbulbs.com

- *Garden Gate*
  subscriptions@augusthome.com
  1–800–341–4768
  PO Box 842
  Des Moines, Iowa 50304

- *White Flower Farm*
  Whiteflowerfarm.com
  1–800–503–9624

Books published by Stackpole Publishing, Inc. and available through *Rug Hooking* Magazine at *www.rughookingmagazine.com*

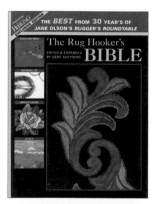

The Rug Hookers Bible,
Gene Shepherd

*Sculpted Rugs in
Waldoboro Style,*
Jacqueline Hansen

*Prodded Hooking for a
Three-Dimensional Effect,*
Gene Shepherd

Shading Flowers,
Jeanne Field

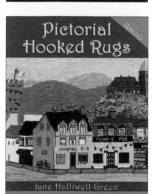

Pictorial Hooked Rugs,
Jane Halliwell Green

Hooked Rug Landscapes
Anne-Marie Littenberg